"Everyone has their personal journey, and most life lessons are difficult. Terri tells her life story as if she's sitting with you as a very close girlfriend. Her story is real life, exciting, heartfelt, and feisty. I found myself smiling, living her story and laughing with her. Mostly, I found a story that I can personally relate to, understanding the underlying reasons why I am the way I am. Thank you, Terri!"

~Lisza Gulyas, Writer and Speaker, Colorado

"If you only read one book this year, this should be it. Terri's story of grit, determination, and gratitude will inspire you to embrace whatever challenge you might be going through—to take a deep breath and begin again!"

~June Ryan RADM, U.S. Coast Guard (ret.)

"Such an inspiring journey of joy, pain, triumph, and passion. Terri's story is full of the emotions most of us feel throughout our lifetime, expressed in such a beautiful way that captures your attention and heart right from the beginning. An extraordinary account of events that led Terri to find her true calling amidst life challenges and circumstances."

~Claudia Niedzielski, Bestselling Author, Entrepreneur, Certified Jack Canfield Success Principles Trainer and Coach

"There is a point in life where reflection of its lessons can be proffered to assist others in their own journey. Terri Mongait has written a beautiful book about the unique, varied, and sundry events in her life. This book will move the reader through her words to reflect upon their understanding of the meaning of their own events . . . and perhaps to 'begin again.'"
~Melisa Pearce CEO and Founder of Touched by a Horse, Inc. and Equine Gestalt Coaching Method Certification Program

"Finding True Purpose is an engaging and heartfelt story of a women's determination to overcome self-limiting beliefs and recognize her true purpose in the aftermath of a near death experience. Not all survivors of a traumatic brain injury (TBI) have the courage and support systems Terri did then—and still does—to get up, shake off the experience, and face new life challenges. Truly inspiring, Terri's journey after the Disney Castle is proof that no matter what life throws at us, we have a choice about how we respond. And yes, we can all begin again. I invite you to do the same.
~Margaret W., Chief Marketing Officer at Mile High Virtual Assistant, LLC, Denver CO
www.milehighvirtualassistant.com

FINDING *True Purpose*

LIFE BEYOND the CASTLE

Terri Mongait, EGC, CCT

Finding True Purpose: Life Beyond the Castle
Published by Victoria and Albert Press
Sedalia, CO

This book is a memoir. It is my story and to the best of my knowledge the events shared in this book are as they occurred. Many of the people in the book are named, and a few of the names have been changed to maintain privacy. Names and identifying details of all clients have been changed to protect the privacy of individuals. The people in this book continue on their journeys and I am grateful for the moment their journey touched mine. If there are any mistakes I do most humbly apologize.

Publisher's Cataloging-in-Publication data

Names: Mongait, Terri, author.
Title: Finding true purpose : life beyond the castle. / by Terri Mongait.
Description: First trade paperback original edition. | Sedalia [Colorado] : Victoria and Albert Press, 2021. | Also published as an ebook.
Identifiers: ISBN 978-1-7347792-0-2
Subjects: LCSH: Autobiography. | Self-actualization (Psychology).
BISAC: BIOGRAPHY & AUTOBIOGRAPHY / Personal Memoirs. | BODY, MIND & SPIRIT / Inspiration & Personal Growth.
Classification: LCC BF575.S37 2021 | DDC 920.9 MONGAIT–dc22

Cover and Interior Design by Victoria Wolf, wolfdesignandmarketing.com

QUANTITY PURCHASES: Schools, companies, professional groups, clubs, and other organizations may qualify for special terms when ordering quantities of this title. For information, contact@victoriaandalbertpress.com.

VICTORIA & ALBERT
PRESS

*For all women and girls struggling to understand
the choices they have made, may they identify, acknowledge,
and remove the negative messages written on
their personal whiteboards.*

WHAT NEXT?
AN INTRODUCTION

Continue to pursue your dreams
and you will persevere.

WALT DISNEY ONCE SAID, "It all started with a mouse." And for me, it did.

Except it really didn't. Nor did it end there.

I began my career working as a full-time, four-handed dental assistant, having been trained as a dental assistant by my boyfriend's mom during my senior year in high school. It was only natural to get a full-time position after graduation.

I next jumped on the chance to work in New York City, first as a receptionist and then as an executive secretary for the National

Basketball Association's vice president of media relations. I stayed with the NBA for two years. After that, I was invited to interview for the position of executive assistant to both the CEO and the general manager of the New Jersey Nets. I was certainly establishing myself as a top-level assistant, and it felt good to be approached for advancement. This was also when I moved out on my own and relocated to a different state for the first time.

After a few years with the Nets, a friend recommended me to interview at a prestigious New York law firm. I initially worked for an attorney who was the department head of trusts and estates. While he was on sabbatical, I substituted in various departments. Because of my exemplary work ethic and all-around excellent secretarial skills (I was one of only a few who actually still took shorthand), I was invited by human resources to interview with the head of the litigation department.

After all the bouncing around I had done—at least to me it felt like bouncing around—I realized that in actuality, I was gaining real-life work experience to prepare me for the "next opportunity," whatever that might be. Each of the positions I held afforded me many experiences to grow, expand, and get a glimmer of my self-worth.

I especially enjoyed working in the heart of New York City. I got to travel into the city, taking the train to the station in Hoboken, New Jersey, and then another train under the Hudson River to the World Trade Center. In the beginning, I took the subway and walked the last few blocks to my building. Once the law firm moved their offices near Battery Park, it was only a train to the World Trade Center and a walk to my office—a grand way to commute to a job.

During my tenure at the law firm, I honed my secretarial skills further and added "legal assistant" to my resume. Working for the head of the litigation department put me at the top of the food chain—the class system typical of most every law firm. Working at a prestigious New York law firm certainly was exciting and educational.

Every department had its own law "language," depending on the area of legal expertise, and I'd had the opportunity to learn many of those languages during the time I substituted in various departments. When I landed in the crowning jewel of litigation, not only did it have its own language, but I became well-versed in state and federal laws, as well as court procedure.

All was going along well until, in 1991, I was faced with a major crossroads moment—I could choose to ignore what was being offered to me because it was a big deal and scary, or I could embrace an unexpected opportunity in spite of my concerns.

One of our most prominent clients was The Walt Disney Company. Early in 1991, my boss made an unanticipated trip to California—unanticipated to me because we did not have any immediate litigation demands on behalf of Disney. When he returned, he informed me that Disney had offered him a position, and he would be heading to California. Because of the personal and professional respect we had for each other, he offered to make me part of his relocation package and be moved, at no cost to me, to Los Angeles to be cast in a role supporting someone in the upper executive levels of The Walt Disney Company ("cast member" is *Disney speak* for "employee," no matter what position you were in).

With this offer on the table, I could either stay in New York, be assigned to a different attorney, and keep the status quo in my current position, *or* I could close my eyes, take a deep breath, lean into the opportunity, and *begin again* in California at the top of The Walt Disney Company. That choice meant moving clear across the country, leaving family, and, most importantly, leaving my boyfriend and not knowing how that decision would affect our relationship. After careful consideration (i.e., trusting my gut), I chose the latter, which would grant me the opportunity to explore my love of "all things Disney" from the vantage point at the top of the Disney castle.

When I was a little girl, I was obsessed with many of the Disney characters, but most especially Mickey Mouse, Peter Pan, and Tinker Bell. I absolutely knew for sure that Peter was going to fly through my window and take me to Neverland. In fact, even though I shared a room with my sister, Claudia, I made sure that my bed was always closest to the window so Peter could find me first.

Every afternoon at four o'clock, I would sit in front of our black-and-white TV and watch *The Mickey Mouse Club*, wishing fervently that I had my own set of Mickey ears. Listening to the opening roll call ... "Darlene ... Bobby ... Sharon ... Jimmy ... and Annette," I was certain that one day they would say, "Terri."

On Sunday nights, my family would get together to watch *The Wonderful World of Disney*, hosted by Walt Disney himself. This was a special time for me because I could lose myself in the fantasy of the story being spun on the TV by Mr. Disney and pretend I was a part of that story. For me, this was a weekly ritual of dreaming about possibilities for my life. Was it fantasy? Maybe. But maybe it was the precursor to what might happen in my future.

Childhood drifted away, along with those childhood dreams. Eventually I was an adult making my own way in the world, far away from the place where I grew up. It was a long road, sometimes challenging but always educational, that took me from Queens, New York, to Manhattan, to Rutherford, New Jersey, and back to Manhattan, before I actually arrived at the top of the castle in the Magic Kingdom. By leaning into the opportunities that presented themselves, that little girl who loved "all things Disney" ended up not only working at The Walt Disney

Company, but eventually working in the upper echelon of The Walt Disney Company.

To top it off, in 1992 I finally married my very own Peter. He didn't fly through my window but showed up via a telephone dating service. He and I almost missed out on meeting each other, as he was twenty minutes late for our first date, but for some reason, I decided to wait just a little bit longer. I'm so very glad I did because we've been together for almost thirty years.

After my boss left Disney in October 2000 to return to private law practice, I stayed on for another year and a half. At that point I realized I did not fit in with the new regime, and I was no longer happy and thriving. It was time to leave the castle and find something that would make me feel fulfilled once again. Coming to the decision that I needed to leave Disney was especially painful since I thought I'd found my dream job and had never planned to leave.

As I tried to figure out "What's next?" (even going back to work for my former boss at his private law firm for a while), I began to question what I was meant to do. What was my true purpose? It wasn't until I sustained a traumatic brain injury that my life and my purpose came into clearer focus. That "opportunity" certainly gave me the time I needed to figure out what the next life chapter might look like.

As I began to recover, the neuro docs presented me with information about what I probably would and would not be able to accomplish after I was "completely" healed. Somehow, I knew it was ultimately my choice to either accept what they told me and believe I would always be "broken" or call *bullshit* on their prognosis and create a wonderful and successful life for myself. I chose the latter.

The long and winding road to the top of the Mouse House and beyond was filled with many opportunities, challenges, strategic choices, and even missteps. Every move and new direction happened as a result of my internal wisdom. Each decision to *begin again* occurred in spite of (or maybe because of) the internal messages written on the blank slate of who I became during my formative years as a child—those messages that had been written on my internal whiteboard.

If you have ever written something on a whiteboard and erased it, then wrote it again and erased it, then repeated writing and erasing over and over, at some point, no matter how much you erase, you can still see the letters on the whiteboard. In the same way, those messages from childhood get written into our psyche and remain with us throughout our lives, unless we acknowledge that they are there, embrace them, and transform them into messaging that serves us and the life we desire. If we try to deny them, they will continue to influence our lives through their subtle, faded letters.

And if we attempt to reject them, they will continue to rewrite their messages with bold markers on our internal whiteboards.

I've come to know we all have messages that were written on our blank slates, our personal whiteboards, when we were young. For me, those messages included statements like: "You'll never be first," "You have to buy your way into being included," and "You are not worth the time or effort for others to be close friends with you." The reality of being the second girl, the middle child, and not the long-awaited boy played a large role in my sense of self-worth and self-esteem. I was clearly not essential and not special. Rather than deny the existence of these internal messages or simply try to avoid them, I learned that the only way for them not to control my life was to acknowledge them. As a result, those messages helped me become who I am today. I was able to embrace them, thank them for the lessons they taught me, and eventually let them go, replacing them with my soul messaging that still serves me today.

Since, for the most part, I had been comfortable being by myself and having only a few close friends, many of the decisions I made in my life were easy. Because it was *just me*, there were times when I said, "Well, why not? What have I got to lose? Besides, just like Wendy going off with Peter to Neverland, it will be an adventure."

Embracing the opportunities presented to me turned out to be a way of lifting up my self-esteem and my sense of self-worth. Going to work for Disney and moving to California had been a risky move, but what did I have to lose at the time? And because of my many experiences with beginning again, when the time came, I was able to connect with my internal courage and conviction to move beyond a traumatic brain injury into a passion-filled life. This journey led me to a life beyond my wildest dreams, from the top of a castle to a grounded life on a ranch with a small herd of horses who help me show people how they can heal and live a purpose-filled life—a life for which I am thankful each and every day.

My journey took me from the East Coast to the West Coast to the mountains of Colorado; from a dental assistant to a legal assistant to an executive assistant; and from a brain-injured patient to a joy-filled ranch owner and equine life coach. My intention is that by sharing my journey, you will see the possibilities within your own life. No matter what you've experienced, no matter what you've lived through, it is possible to find your way to the life of your dreams ... and beyond.

PART ONE

Identifying the Messages

CHAPTER 1

Middle Child

*All that makes me unique are the
things that make me ME.*

BORN IN 1957 IN QUEENS VILLAGE, New York, I grew up
in middle-class America. For the first four years of my life, I was
the second girl. Then, my brother was born. It seemed to me that
now I really wasn't special.

Basically, in my mind, I was superfluous. At least that is how
I felt. Never to be "first." Never to be the "only." And, with my
brother's birth, always in the middle. I wore second-best hand-
me-downs; rarely did I receive something new. Second child,
second girl. Always second.

One Christmas, my sister, Claudia, got one of the first Barbie dolls. Santa brought me Midge (Barbie's plain friend). The next year, Claudia got Ken, and I got Skipper (Barbie's little sister). I felt "not good enough" to get a real Barbie. I continued to get the second fiddles—a clear message to my young psyche that I was considered secondary.

Christmas morning always started the same in our home. We had to wait at the top of the stairs, and Dad would go downstairs and plug in the tree. Mom was waiting at the bottom of the stairs with the camera. As soon as the tree was lit, we ran down excitedly.

When I was eleven, Claudia was thirteen, and Chris was seven, and we were all very excited for Santa's arrival. Claudia and I knew about Santa, but Chris was still on the cusp, or pretending not to know so he could continue to rake in the holiday loot. The first gifts I saw on this particular Christmas morning were three bicycles. A brand-new boy's Stingray bike, which was obviously for my brother; my sister's old bike, all cleaned up; and a new English Racer with skinny wheels and gears. This totally confused me. *Chris got a new bike, Claudia got her bike all fixed and shiny, but what about the other one? Did Dad get a bike?* I certainly couldn't picture my mom peddling around on a street bike. What about me? Where was my bike? I wanted to cry.

Mom must have seen the confused look on my face. She explained that yes, Santa brought the new boy's bike for Chris, since he obviously couldn't ride a girl's bike. Claudia got the new

English Racer bike because she was getting too big for her old bike, and Santa had fixed and cleaned up Claudia's bike for me. Now everyone had a bike. I sniffled back my tears and stuffed my hurt down deep and pretended to be thrilled with my bike. But what I learned was that once again I was the one not worth being given something new.

Another gift that beat my butt for many years was a very special puppet. I desperately wanted Lamb Chop, the lamb puppet on *The Shari Lewis Show*. But Claudia got Lamb Chop, and I got Charlie Horse (Lamb Chop's sidekick). Second once again.

I will share here that just last year, my husband saw a Lamb Chop plush toy at a dog show and bought one for me. Almost fifty years later, I finally got my Lamb Chop. And thinking about it now that I live on a ranch and work with horses, maybe my mom had been right: Charlie Horse was the best choice for me. But at the time, I felt hurt to always be second.

As a child, I was an extreme introvert, although I didn't learn that term until decades later. How that showed up for me was that I was very quiet. Some would call me shy. And I was never first to raise my hand in school, even though I usually knew the answer. What I did know is that I preferred to be alone. I would choose to play with one friend rather than a big party of twenty or more. That scenario completely overwhelmed me.

Although I liked being alone, I didn't like feeling left out. At home, I was pretty much left on my own to do my own thing.

Most of the time, rather than feeling that my family was giving me space, it felt like I was invisible to everyone else in the house. Those feelings forced me to rely on myself and be okay with being alone, even when I didn't necessarily want it.

For instance, when I was around nine, even though I was old enough to play outside, there wasn't anyone my age in the neighborhood. So while my sister and brother were off with their friends, I found ways to entertain myself.

There were no carpools or playdates during this era and no focus on trying to bring children together to play. Whomever you lived near and could walk to—those were your friends. With no one my age to play with, my sister didn't want her little sister tagging along, and I didn't want to play army games with the boys. I ended up by myself with a book or in the closet with some of my toys—and I'm not talking the big walk-in closets of today. This was a small bedroom closet where I had to push the shoes out of my way, and the clothes hung down and cast shadows from my flashlight.

Usually I pretended I was on a lifeboat and I had to take care of my stuffed animals, which I preferred to play with rather than my dolls. It was a lot of responsibility to be the caretaker for all my stuffed animals, but I knew I could do it. After all, I took pretty good care of myself, didn't I? In the dark closet, I was safe, out of the way, and comfortable. And I was in charge of what happened.

Being the second daughter and the middle child, I definitely fulfilled the definition of "middle child." According to health-guidance.com, some of the most common characteristics of being a middle child include low self-esteem, jealousy, feelings of emptiness or inadequacy, and a tendency to be introverted. Middle children are also known to be the peacemakers. And considering my mom's propensity to discourage fighting of any kind, this was right up my alley. We were taught not to share feelings, emotions, and especially differences of opinion (in fact, it was not okay to share any opinion). In my family, we did not deconstruct feelings and emotions. And we did not fight ... ever!

Sharing a room with my sister, we both learned that if we had an argument or disagreement, one of us needed to leave the room and never discuss it again. We were taught that if we had a disagreement with anyone in the family and were unable to negotiate peace, the only other way to handle it was to walk away, leave the room, and never ever discuss it. Therefore, nothing was ever talked about, concluded, or resolved. It was ignored.

Certainly not having a healthy way of fighting or discussing an issue was problematic throughout my growing up. And later on, this way of dealing with conflict drove my husband crazy, as his family discusses issues to the tiniest detail. One time we were having a disagreement, and I got up to leave the room. He gently prevented me from leaving until we talked things through. I love him for having the patience and understanding to help me learn how to have a healthy debate. With him, I learned that it's okay to agree to disagree—and no one is going to be harmed or die when you do.

As a child, I loved being outside in nature. I was much more comfortable with animals than with people. While I did not have a lot of experience with little children, I did find out that if I was asked to hold a baby, it would fuss and start to cry. But if I had the opportunity to hold a puppy or kitten, it would curl up and fall asleep.

This early time in my life was when I fell in love with books. I could lose myself in the story. And I usually had more than one book going at all times. I remember one evening when I was out in the backyard in my tree cave, reading *Little Women*. As I normally did, I brought my book and a stuffed animal and headed over to the honeysuckle bush in the back corner of our yard. I pushed the front branches aside to reveal a perfect cave of roots and leaves, space enough for me and my cherished possessions. It was a quiet sanctuary where I could be alone with my book. Just enough sunlight seeped in through the vines, and the wonderful, sweet scent of honeysuckle enveloped me.

On this particular evening, I was called in for dinner and, oh my, I didn't want to stop reading. The characters were about to have a party, and I didn't want to miss it. *Just a few more minutes*, I thought to myself. *Please!* My mom was insistent that I come in *now*. Luckily, when I finished dinner and was able to return to my book, I realized that the party was still waiting for me and

I was able to join the festivities as I continued reading. What a fabulous realization! The characters in my books waited for me to return before continuing on with their story. How wonderful to have my presence be so valuable.

Another characteristic of middle children is that they tend to feel unseen. Feeling invisible was certainly true for me. This meant I was not worth being seen, and as a consequence, I never wanted to draw attention to myself. I accomplished this in various ways. In school, we frequently had spelling bees. The entire class had to line up against the wall, and one at a time we were given a word to spell. If you got it correct, you got to go to the back of the line for another attempt until there was a winner. While I was smart and knew the word I was given, usually by the third time through the line, I would misspell the word on purpose just so I could sit down, which accomplished my need to be unseen.

Every so often, my need to be unseen was tested by the Universe. For instance, my Catholic church held a special event every May. Since May is the month of Our Lady and my school was Our Lady of Lourdes, they held a special event after each of the Sunday masses. My school was taught by Dominican nuns, and one of the events was a celebration of the different levels required to become a professed Dominican nun. Three girls were always chosen from the first grade classes to portray each level of education and vows. Each of the three girls dressed in the attire that represented one of the three professions—novitiate, first vows, and professed Dominican nun.

During my first grade year, I was chosen (more like volunteered by my mom because standing up in front of the entire congregation to give a speech is not something I would ever volunteer to do) to be the professed Dominican nun and dress in the full Dominican habit. At that time, Dominican sisters dressed in a white tunic with a leather belt and a large rosary. They wore a mantle, which was a black cape or a coat that was an expression of the penitential spirit of the congregation. A black veil covered the head.

I had to stand up in front of the entire religious congregation and recite a paragraph about all my education and what I had to go through to become a professed Dominican sister. I thought this would be pure torture for me. I hated practicing and dreaded the upcoming event.

The day of the event, I was a trembling mess until I started dressing in my nun's habit. I still have the picture of me in a full Dominican habit. Memorizing all I had to recite turned out not to be difficult, but I thought getting up in front of a crowd would be awful. And yet, when it came time to stand up and recite my speech in full costume, I found that I loved it, and I was good at it too. Imagine that! Dressing up in costume gave me the illusion of being someone other than me. Someone worth listening to and paying attention to. You see, it was not Terri in front of the crowd, reciting the speech and taking the vows. No, it was Sister Mary Theresa who they were all looking at and listening to. Putting on the Dominican habit and standing up in front of the crowd gave me the feeling of being accepted and that what I had to say was worthwhile.

I did not have many friends in school, so I pretty much stayed by myself. Around fourth or fifth grade, I started to socialize more. Since after school was time for homework, maybe a little TV, then bed, I didn't really get together with friends during the week. The only time I could hang out with a friend was during lunch at school or on the weekends—and only if I could get a ride from a parent or walk to a friend's house.

I found that if I did not make plans at school on Friday to get together on the weekend with someone, it did not happen, because making plans from home was almost impossible. The main phone at home was in the kitchen, and there was no privacy. If I wanted to use the phone, it meant that I and my conversation were in the middle of people coming and going. We also had one in the hallway upstairs. Yet, there was no place to take that phone and chat either. The cord only went so far and did not reach my bedroom. Not at all conducive to "girl talk."

I remember having two good girlfriends during my last years in grammar school: Mary and Tara. Tara and I became close first.

We were very much alike. Same grades, same shyness. Then Mary joined our little group. Mary was my "who I want to be" friend. She was just one step above me in my mind. If I got a 95 on a test, she got 100. She always had her hand up first to answer a question. She was an only child and had great clothes (a regular fashionista of the 1960s). She also lived in an apartment and had her own room—which was so cool to me, the second daughter in a family of five who shared her room with her sister and lived in a house with one bathroom.

The three of us were very close. We even had a crush on the same teacher, although I guess most of the prepubescent girls had a crush on Mr. Demico. Especially in a Catholic school run by nuns. Almost every Saturday, the three of us would get together at one of our houses for a day of play. We would take turns at each other's house and decide whether it would include a sleepover.

One Saturday, I called Tara to find out what we were doing, and her mom told me that Tara had already gone out with Mary. *Wait! What, without me? Not even telling me why? Did I miss something? Did I offend one of them? Did I forget what the plan was? It must be my fault.* I didn't know what had happened or why. But I felt awful. *Why didn't they want me along? Why didn't they tell me anything? Why was I not included?* So many questions I could not answer and was too afraid to ask. I was confused and hurt. And I felt alone and left out. I didn't understand why this had happened and could not process the feelings of not being included.

I never did find out why. And I never asked. I assumed they finally realized that my friendship was not worth it. I also never played with them again. I ignored them at school. I did not want to appear like I was begging for their friendship, so I took a deep breath and moved on. For a reason I would never know, they had excluded and rejected me. As a result, I did what had become a coping mechanism for me when I found myself left out or ignored and unseen. I had a short cry. No wailing or bawling because that would have brought attention. It was just a few tears by myself. Afterward, I blew my nose and wiped away the tears. Then I grabbed a book and went off on another literary journey. I was safe and accepted in the pages of a book.

You would think I could have gone to my mom and found some comfort, or at least some plausible explanation that would assuage my feelings of being inadequate, ostracized, and left out. Unfortunately, my mom was not the "come here and let me give you a hug and we'll make it all better" mom. I don't ever remember sitting or cuddling on either of my parents' laps. No reading of a bedtime story. No "tell me all about your day" or "how does that make you feel?" No, I was on my own and had to try to figure it out myself or do my best to ignore what happened and move on.

Once, when we were on vacation at Otsego Lake in upstate New York, it was early evening, and I was outside with my cousin Tim. This was always the perfect time of day for me: fireflies flitting about, crickets chirping, just enough evening light to see some clouds drift across the sky. Tim and I walked quietly down to the dock. By this time, it was dark, and the lake was calm and quiet. The fireflies were out and twinkling in the night air. I remember practicing skipping rocks, which was apparently an important skill to have for a ten-year-old girl.

Tim decided it would be a good idea to sit in one of the boats that were tied up at the dock. Because these were not our boats, I was hesitant to agree. But I figured as long as we didn't untie the boat and drift off, we were okay. He got in the boat first. I hesitated momentarily to join him. The only apprehension I had was, again, that it was not our boat. But I had gotten in boats before, so getting in was no big deal. I had one foot on the dock and one on the boat when I suppose Tim thought he would be funny. He pushed the boat away from the dock just as I was ready to shift my weight toward the boat. My legs split wide, and I didn't know which way to fall, so I pulled both legs in and fell into the lake. Since I could swim well, I surfaced almost immediately, realizing that he was in the boat laughing his ass off. I swam around to the dock ladder, climbed out, and walked back to the cabin.

My shorts and top were dripping as I walked, and I could hear the sound of my sneakers squishing with each step I took. Crying, wet, and feeling hurt that he would play a trick on me and think it was funny, I couldn't understand why he'd done it. *Why did he think that was so funny? Had it been his plan all along to make me fall in the lake? And didn't he realize it wouldn't be funny to me since I could have been hurt, and I was definitely embarrassed?*

By the time I made it back home, I was still crying. Through my tears, I told my mom what had happened, and all she said to me was, "What's the big deal? It's only water, and you know how to swim. Go dry off and go to bed." That was it. In essence, "Put on your big girl panties and get over it." A valuable childhood message and lesson I learned well. Stuff your feelings down because they don't matter; don't look at them and certainly don't let them control your life!

Another valuable lesson I learned as a young girl with low self-esteem and an "I'm not enough" syndrome was the value of currency. I discovered that in some instances, I could buy my way into being included. Every summer, we spent two weeks at Otsego Lake. One summer, my sister's friend Suzanne was finally old enough to drive her family's boat. It was a flat-bottomed boat called a Boston Whaler, and it went super-fast, skipping over the tops of the waves. Since Suzanne could now drive the boat, she and my sister frequently went out on the lake. Of course, Claudia didn't want her little sister hanging around with them, so I was not included. After listening to Claudia talk about how they wanted to go out on the lake the next day but didn't have money to buy gas, I knew I had a way in. I realized that if I offered to pay for either a pizza for lunch or a tank of gas for the boat, I would be permitted to "belong." I could buy my way into joining them for an afternoon. It worked, so I continued to offer to pay. This did not happen every day while we were on vacation, but when it did, I was able to spend the time with my sister, speeding along faster than I thought possible, bouncing off the waves, and trying not to fall out.

One of the most magical experiences while we were out on the lake was when we stopped to just hang out in the middle of the water. Every once in a while, a storm would sprout up. If the conditions were right, we could watch the curtain of rain move toward us as it crossed the lake. Just before it hit, Suzanne would fire up the engine, and we would try to outrun the storm. It was exciting, exhilarating, and scary all at the same time. Well worth the price of admission.

CHAPTER 2

You'll Get Over It

*Loss is inevitable. It's how you respond
that makes you grow.*

I DON'T REMEMBER EVER SEEING my parents have an argument. No fighting, screaming, yelling, or even raised voices. Mom was acquiescent. She did what she had to do to keep the peace and not make waves. Dad worked long hours in Manhattan and took on overtime whenever he could. I learned early on that one did everything one could not to anger Dad. I remember one time when Claudia and I were fighting in the hall upstairs, and Mom came over to us, clearly upset. "Don't fight, don't raise your voices. Dad will get mad. Now make up and stop fighting."

On Saturdays, when he was home attempting to accomplish a much-needed home repair project, my siblings and I would get up, eat quickly, and get the hell out of the house before he started. What would usually set him off was if my brother, Chris, had used his tools and forgotten to put them back. I knew not to be around when that happened.

Dad could be a stern disciplinarian, but at times he was also a great team leader. For instance, we were the only family on the block with a pool, and every year it was a family project to set it up. Although it was hard and tedious work, I really enjoyed the project, as there was a fabulous goal, and we all worked together. My dad would dig up the ground, and we would take an old window screen and sift the entire area where the pool liner was to go. "No rocks!" Dad reminded us every year. Even a small pebble could puncture the liner and cause a leak. I knew that fixing a leak under water was no small accomplishment, so I took his instruction to heart as we cleared the area.

It certainly was fun being out in the yard under the spring sun, working together to get the project completed. It was a time when I didn't need to spend all day reading or trying to figure out how to be included.

There were also other times when I wasn't totally excluded within the family either. For instance, on hot evenings, late at night, my sister and I could hear Mom and Dad in the pool. Claudia and I had the back bedroom, and we could see them floating around. "Mom?" we would call out softly. And most times the response was, "Sure, put your suits on and come on down and don't wake your brother."

We got to float around, cool off on the hot New York summer nights, and get a lesson in astronomy. "That constellation is Annie's Arm," my dad would share. We didn't need to know that there was no such thing. I thought, *How cool is it that ... a constellation is named after my mom?*

When Dad worked overtime, usually on a Friday night, he would come home late with Chinese food. We kids were supposed to be asleep, but we knew it was Friday night and there was a good possibility that Dad would be stopping for Chinese takeout, so we would sit on the top of the stairs and wait for Mom and Dad to sit in the living room and begin to enjoy their meal. We would then make little noises so they would know that we were still awake. Mom always ordered an extra egg roll that Claudia and I would get to share.

Eventually, I had a best friend, and her name was Debbie. I met her over our back fence. Debbie would stand at the fence and watch us in the pool. One summer day, I asked my mom if I could invite her to swim. After that, we became inseparable. We stayed at each other's house every weekend. We played make-believe together—*Lost in Space* was a favorite. This was the original *Lost in Space* from the 1960s. We would re-create the episodes as best we could and trade off playing Penny and Will (because they were the best characters). We always made Debbie's little sister, Diane, play Penny's pet alien monkey (the monkey's name was Debbie the Bloop after the only sound it made: bloop). I'm not sure Diane ever forgave us for that experience.

We rarely played Barbies. Instead, we played with Liddle Kiddles. Liddle Kiddles were introduced in 1966. They were tiny dolls, ranging from two and a half to three and a half inches tall, with poseable limbs and rooted hair. Designed to resemble children in neighborhoods across America, different hairstyles and painted facial features made them unique. There were so many different ones, including Bunson Burnie (a fireman), Calamity Jiddle (a cowgirl), Howard Biff Boodle (the little boy), and Kampy Kiddle (the tomboy). I had all twenty-four of them. And I loved each one. I also had a special case to carry them in, and I took them everywhere. They were my best friends.

Unfortunately, one time coming back from vacation at Debbie's, I forgot and left my Liddle Kiddles behind in her dad's car. The next day, I called and asked to come over to get my dolls. She told me the car had been stolen. Oh my god, my Kiddles were gone! Another relationship ripped away from me. I felt devastated and abandoned. And yet this feeling and the scenario that followed were not unfamiliar. I was not comforted by my mom, nor did I get my Kiddles back or replaced. When I told Mom, her response was, "They're just dolls. You'll get over it." So I mourned by myself and then moved on. That is what I had learned. You don't share your feelings, and you don't lament over the loss. Looking back, I see a recurring theme throughout my early life, one that followed me into my adult life as well.

Debbie and I were so very close that the day her cat was giving birth to kittens, she called me and told me to come over right away. I ran like the dickens to get there in time. The cat, Mittens, was in a box with towels and two new lives. And then another one started coming out. Wow, I had not expected that! I had no idea this is what giving birth was like. *OUCH! Yuck! Eww!* But I was fascinated. And Mittens was such a good mom. She cleaned them up and made sure her new kittens were doing fine and finding their way to a teat for nourishment.

Every summer, I spent a week with Debbie and her family at their rental house, and she came with us to upstate New York for our vacation. With her family, I experienced what a close, loving mom was like. It was a very different experience for me. I was jealous of Debbie for having such a loving mom who asked about her day and was involved with projects and what was going on in all her children's lives. I saw firsthand how much love Debbie's mom showed toward her children and how much they loved her. I felt guilty for not feeling that way about my mom.

I remember one occasion with Debbie at their vacation house

when we were out bike riding. No helmets or kneepads were used back then. We were going down a steep hill (or so it seemed from my perspective), and I fell. Badly. Debbie raced home to get her mom. They showed up in the car, and her mom helped me up and got me in the car so I wouldn't have to walk. Debbie took the bike home. Once we got to their house, Debbie's mom sat me in the kitchen, dried my tears, and began to clean my skinned knees. Making sure there were no rocks or dirt in the wounds, she then put on some iodine and bandaged me up. How wonderful it was to be cared for like that! I'd never had anyone put my needs first.

It was a revelation to discover that not every family was like mine. Both of Debbie's parents were engaged in their kids' lives. Her father was always doing something with Joey, Debbie's brother, and her mother was constantly involved with something either Debbie or her sisters, Laurie and Diane, were doing. I treasured my time with Debbie and her family, and I know we spent more time at her house than we did at mine.

It was hard not to compare moms. My mom was loving in her own way and she took care of our basic needs, but there was no over-involvement in anything we kids did. When she did spend time with any of us, it seemed she spent more time with Chris than with Claudia or me. And there was never much hugging or consoling when we needed it. She had more of a stoic, "That's the way it is, move on" attitude. By getting to spend more time at Debbie's house, I began to see what was missing in my own family.

My mom was distant and seemed to go through the motions of the day without much emotion—ours or hers.

My mom did not work when I was growing up, but she volunteered at our school a few times per week as a lunch lady. And she was a den leader for Chris's Cub Scout pack. Because Mom didn't work outside of our home, I could always count on her to be home when I returned from school. Yet, even though she was there physically, most of the time she was distant, uninterested in what had happened during my day, smoking like a fiend, and involved in some project or preparing dinner. Since that was the way it was, I was content to do my homework at the dining room table with Chris and Claudia. After homework, we would disperse until dinnertime.

Much later in life, I would come to realize that Mom was a functioning alcoholic. I certainly did not know anything about family alcoholism at the time. Never did I see my mom walking around with a bottle of vodka. This was the early 1960s, and every adult drank. In fact, Mom would meet Dad at the door with a drink in her hand for him when he came home from work. It was normal. At least it was normal for me.

My earliest memory of there being something wrong was a time when I was in the kitchen one afternoon. No one else was around, and I wanted a glass for my juice. Being a somewhat athletic kid (at least I thought so), I was not going to pull over a chair, climb up, and get my glass. No, it was more fun to jump up, use my arms as leverage, do a quick full-body turn, and plant my butt on the kitchen counter. Ha! Success. I opened the cabinet door, and there was Mom's "glass of water" high out of reach. I remember there always being a glass of water on the high shelf in the cabinet.

Well, I was thirsty and there was water. So I grabbed the glass, and just as I was about to take a drink, Mom came in and yelled at me to put it down. It wasn't mine, what was I doing, and on and on she ranted. Pretty extreme reaction over a glass of water. She really scared me, and I nearly fell off the counter. It made no sense, and I didn't understand what the big deal was over a glass of water. I put down her glass, got an empty glass, jumped down, poured my juice, and left the kitchen. What I came to know as true many, many years later was that it was not Mom's glass of water—it was her glass of vodka, which she sipped on all afternoon.

Toward the end of my eighth grade year, Debbie told me that her dad was building a house in New Jersey where they had been renting every year, and they would be moving there. She would be going to high school in New Jersey. Because of the lesson learned earlier in my life with Mary and Tara, I immediately cut her off. I had to protect my broken heart. I barely even said goodbye. I was being left behind by another good friend, and she was taking away my second Mom. It really hurt.

Since I had no idea how to process my emotions, and I had no one to talk to about them, I did what I had done before. I just cut off the relationship and moved on. I was going to high school, too, so goodbye. No big deal. Life goes on. Good luck. I had been taught early and frequently that you did not express your emotions, especially hurt or sadness, as it was a sign of weakness. You stuffed them down and moved on. So that's exactly what I did.

CHAPTER 3

Moving Into Adulthood

*Yesterday is your memory and tomorrow
is your possibility.*

HIGH SCHOOL. Now things would be different. New friends,
new location. I even had to take two city buses to get to school.
I went in hoping I could be different by making new friends and
not being on my own so much.

I walked into the building that first day, excited about all the
possibilities. I told myself it wasn't so scary—everyone else in my
grade was new too. Level playing field, right? In fact, I reminded
myself that I actually had a leg up because my sister was going to

this same school, and she was a junior. Her being an upperclass-man was my "ace in the hole" ... or so I thought. She did introduce me to some of her friends, but I came to realize rather quickly that juniors did not hang out with freshmen. I was on my own.

There was more to the story, too, so let me give some back-ground: Claudia and I were very different. In high school, my sister was the pretty one with long blond hair and many friends; I was the one with a short "pixie cut," a hairstyle that had gone out of fashion more than a decade earlier, and no friends. She was trendy and tried to stay on top of fashion changes as best she could. During this time of "the Farrah" hairstyle, after Farrah Fawcett from *Charlie's Angels*, my hair was not in style and it certainly didn't put me in the cool clique.

I was not interested in making sure I had on the right makeup, but I did attempt to grow out my hair so I did not look so differ-ent. Luckily, we had to wear a school uniform, so I didn't have to bother with my clothes looking "right." Because my energy was spent elsewhere, hair and makeup or, in my case, a lack thereof, only made me feel more strongly that I did not fit in. Certainly not with the "in" crowd. I was not involved in team sports, so I didn't fit in there either. I fell somewhere in between. At least this was a place and a feeling I was familiar with.

During this first year, I decided to lean into my fear of speak-ing and ran for the only freshman spot on the athletic board. I had great organizational skills, and I thought this would be a good way to be included and belong. How could I have known that it was also a way to reinforce my sense of not being wanted if I lost?

I ran against Erin, a girl who was the athletic one and on almost all of the sports teams. I, on the other hand, was the organized one who was already volunteering as the manager of some of the teams. Of course, one of the athletic teachers was always in charge, but my job was to take care of and clean up the equipment. A huge part of my responsibility was sitting at the officials' table at basketball games and running the scoreboard. Erin and I had slightly different roles, but in my mind, they were equally important. I figured I had as good a shot as anyone.

The only downside: I would have to get up in front of the entire student body and give a speech. Me, the introvert. What could I possibly say in front of the entire student body that would make them vote for me? This time, I would not be dressed up as someone else. I had to make this speech for and about myself. To top it off, there were hundreds of freshmen in my class, plus hundreds more for each of the other three grades—and all would be assembled, listening to and looking at me.

The most challenging part of writing this speech was the fact that it was only a few weeks into the school year. I really didn't know many of my fellow students, and they didn't know me. What could I tell them about me that would earn their vote? What could I possibly say in a few short minutes to convince them that I was worthy?

When it was my turn to speak, I stood up, took a deep breath, and walked over to the podium. I heard my sister yell encouragement, and that voice made me smile and relax. Looking out over the entire student body in the auditorium, I knew Claudia had my back. I wasn't alone.

It wasn't a very long speech. It was only intended to let everyone see and hear from the candidates. I was so glad when it was over. And yet, once again, I realized that not only had I survived, but I'd actually enjoyed it. That was a revelation. I discovered that I didn't need to be dressed in costume as someone else. I could stand up in front of an auditorium of people, most of whom I did not know, and speak with conviction and enthusiasm.

The elections were held the following day, and I lost. I cried in the girls' bathroom by myself. Then I picked myself back up and went to the rest of my classes. There was nothing I could do other than what I'd always done—cry my tears and move on.

The next year, the same thing happened. There was one sophomore spot on the athletic board, and Erin and I ran against each other. I lost again. Why did I keep running? It was because I had paid my dues, or so I thought, by all the volunteer work I had done involving the sports teams and players, and I was desperately seeking inclusion—the stamp of approval of the student body to be elected to the athletic board.

In my junior year, there were finally two spots on the board. I was thrilled. I wouldn't have to run against Erin this time. I went to the current board to submit my candidacy and told them I would be running for whichever spot Erin was not running. To my great surprise, they told me I could not run for the other opening. I *had* to run against Erin. Wow, seriously? WTF? I thought about it for a few minutes and made a decision. *The hell with that!* I thought. *I'm done with doing all the organization work and planning. I'm done with addressing the student body to validate why I was a better choice than the candidate who was totally sports-oriented.* I was not going to put myself through this again. I withdrew my nomination and walked out.

As the team manager, I was involved but always on the periphery, never at the center of the group. As the team manager, I didn't really belong, and I knew I could not "buy" my way into the athletic board clique. The recurring message of not being good enough as myself or valued enough to be considered for the athletic board was familiar, and it stung. Hurt and angry, I decided to quit every team I'd been managing. *I'll show them! I'll leave them hanging to fill all those roles.*

At the time, I did not understand, nor did I inquire about, the real reasons for being left out. I was obviously good enough to do the manager planning, scheduling, and equipment schlepping, but for some unknown reason, I was not being permitted to run for the second position. I found out later that the current board members wanted Erin on the board since she had two years of experience, and they also wanted the co-captain of the varsity basketball team for the other spot. They knew I would lose to Erin but did not know if I would lose to the other nominee for the second spot on the board.

By this point in my young life, the message of "not good enough" had been written on the whiteboard of my soul many times. It was getting harder and harder to erase that message. And when I did erase it, I could still see the words. Etched into the back of my hand like the black punishment quill used by Dolores Umbridge in *Harry Potter*, the message remained.

Once I left the athletic department, I considered what other groups I might possibly join but then decided to just lie low, do my schoolwork, and embrace being a loner. I soon landed in a group of other "outcasts." We didn't fit into any of the typical cliques—cheerleaders, honor society, student council, sports teams, or stoners, so we had our own small group. There was no label for this group of misfits. It was just those of us who didn't fit anywhere else yet longed for a community of some sort. It was here that I was introduced to my very first boyfriend, Tim.

Tim was an enigma. He was captain of the boys' gymnastics team, played Pop Warner football, and, starting in his senior year, became a stoner. In spite of his popularity, he paid attention to me.

During my junior year, I learned that the "buy my way into friendship lesson" from so many years prior at the lake worked for a boyfriend too. Making out was the wonderful new currency of teenage and young adult years. And I scored big time. *Look at me now*, I thought to myself. *I've got the jock and a date for the junior and senior proms.* I felt rather proud of myself. I had finally found a group of friends where I was accepted, and I fit in. As Tim's girlfriend, I was automatically included in his group of friends. It felt really good.

This being the late 1970s, pot played a factor. I did not smoke (yet), but everyone else in the group did. Still, I was included. Not because I was valuable on my own but because I was Tim's girlfriend. At that time of my life, that was just fine with me.

Toward the end of senior year, I realized that I would not be going to college. According to my dad, college for girls was only for those who wanted to become a doctor, lawyer, or some other fancy professional. Otherwise, a girl could be a secretary or work in a store and get whatever position she could until she got married and started a family. He was not going to pay for college for either my sister or me. Girls were not worth an unnecessary college education and expense. Get a job, get married, have babies. That's what was expected. Dad did, however, pay for my brother to attend a community college.

Ironically, years later after her divorce and as a single mom, my sister acquired her nursing degree, and I completed my bachelor's degree in natural health. We each paid for our own college education, and because of my full-time, well-paying job as an administrative assistant, I was financially able to assist Claudia with payment for her final semester. I remember telling her it was not a loan but a grant—payment to be made by taking my blood pressure whenever I visited her.

During my final year in high school, I got a part-time job as a dental assistant, thanks to Tim's mom. I was very excited to be earning my own money, and I thought this extra income, added to my allowance, would enable me to buy new clothes whenever I needed them and not have to ask Mom. Much to my surprise, as soon as I started working, my allowance stopped, and I was charged rent. Seriously? Rent? I was quite annoyed at this new development. Since I was the first child in our home to hold a job while still in school, I had no one to compare notes with. Instead of having additional money to spend like I'd been counting on, my allowance was cut off, and I had to adapt. Mom made the rules and that was that.

Since I was initially only working part-time, the rent was not a lot, but the unfair principle of it felt massive. From then on, a portion of my salary was handed over to Mom. And when I changed jobs and worked full-time after high school, my rent increased too. Instead of receiving praise, or even acknowledgment, for my sense of responsibility and for taking initiative, I had to pay an increase in rent as my earnings went up. It felt like I had to pay to stay in my childhood home—the recurring message of having to pay my way to continue to be included. I don't know that I felt sad or unloved at the time, because it was all that I knew, but I did feel angry, especially since I was the first one of my siblings to get a paying job. It would not have occurred to me to say no to Mom. Even though her rules bothered me, I accepted them.

Because I knew I would not be going to college, my first full-time job after high school was as a "four-handed" dental assistant. This position was the beginning of dental assistants not only prepping and sterilizing equipment and taking and developing X-rays, but also sitting across from the dentist, handing him appropriate tools and instruments, mixing up amalgam for fillings, and cleaning up after the session. It was the cutting edge of the dental assistant field, and I was one of the early assistants trained in this technique in the borough of Queens.

Tim went off to Syracuse University, and we *sort of* had a long-distance relationship. Every Saturday night, one of our friends would come over and pick me up, and we'd hang out and smoke weed (yes, by this time I did inhale). One Saturday night, no one showed up. No phone call to our house phone (this was prior to cell phones), and I was left waiting. Talk about a flashback to my Mary-Tara incident. *What the hell! Again? Really?*

This time I did find out that they didn't want to hang out with me because all I did was talk about Tim. Well, of course, that's what I'd talk about ... duh?!

CHAPTER 4

Working in the Real World

Put on your big girl panties and learn to soar.

MY FIRST FULL-TIME POSITION was at a dental office, but not the one where I had begun working part-time in high school. Unfortunately, that office did not need another full-time assistant, so I applied at a different office and went on my first job interview. Apparently, I had received a good recommendation from the dentist I formerly worked for, and I was offered a full-time position.

In addition to four-handed assisting, I handled all the back-office requirements and ordered all supplies. After a few months, I also made all the night guards with this neat machine using melted plastic and suction to make the impressions. A lot of responsibility for someone right out of high school!

Still living at home, I commuted to my job for almost two years. During that time, little did I know that I would be given the opportunity to work on, practice, and trust my intuition. One of the dentists I worked with really set my *creep meter* on high. I made sure there was always a patient in the dental room with me and that I was never alone with him. I knew that even though I could get my dental work done for free at the office, there would be no nitrous oxide for me ... ever. I felt strongly that I needed to be in control. I remember a holiday office event where one of the other dentists' wives was in attendance, and as the *creep meter* dentist leaned in to give her a holiday kiss, he squeezed her breast. She pulled back, blushing and laughing, but said nothing. I was disgusted and knew it was time for me to move on and think about a new job.

Something I've come to understand about my work life was that rarely, if ever, did I plan out my future. What I did was take advantage of opportunities when they presented themselves. Fortunately, such an opportunity came along almost immediately when I was given the chance to interview for a receptionist job in New York City. If I got the position, I wouldn't need to drive to work any longer. Instead, as a real grown-up, I'd have to take the bus and subway into Manhattan and join the working girl forces in the Big Apple.

At the time, my sister was working as a secretary for a bank in Manhattan. A friend of Claudia's knew I had secretarial training and recommended me as a replacement for her as receptionist for the National Basketball Association. Not being a sports fan, this seemed like any other secretarial position. Most appealing to me initially was that I could leave the dental office. While I was appreciative of being on the cutting edge of dental assisting, I knew deep in my core that I was meant for something bigger, and I needed to find out what that could be. I was excited about taking the next step up in my life and career, and I knew I would be doing that by joining the secretarial forces in Manhattan.

After I went in for the interview, I realized this job was a big deal. The offices were connected to Madison Square Garden, and these were the fanciest offices I had ever been in. The reception area was a large room with plush chairs and a sofa. There were mahogany tables and bookshelves with a smattering of strategic lighting and well-thought-out pictures conveying major basketball stars in various degrees of spectacular game shots. If I got the position, I would be a part of something extraordinary.

The commissioner at the time was Lawrence O'Brien. Mr. O'Brien had been the head of the Democratic National Committee, and it was his office that was broken into during the Nixon-Watergate episode. I would be working with someone who played a huge role in our political history.

I was thrilled to learn that I was hired. As the receptionist, all calls came through me, and I was required to greet each caller with, "National Basketball Association, how may I direct your call?"

Not too long after I started, I walked into the office on a Monday morning, and it appeared that something must have happened over the weekend because my switchboard was lit up like a Christmas tree. I stuffed my coat and purse under my desk and started answering calls as quickly as I could. The callers were irate, and I did my best to reroute them to the appropriate executive. I heard four-letter words I had never heard before. Listening to the fans who called in and having been briefed by our director of security, I found out that there had been a fight at a game, which was alleged to have been racially motivated. This situation was above my pay grade, but I did the best I could. Until …

One fan used such foul language that I had had enough. I interrupted him and said, "Excuse me sir, but they don't pay me enough to listen to your *shit*," before hanging up. Then I called my supervisor, Ken, and told him what I had done. I didn't know if I was going to be reprimanded, or even possibly terminated, but I felt I needed to be honest and own up to what I'd just said. Ken told me that I shouldn't have to deal with irate fans like that and said how sorry he was that I'd had to listen to such an outburst. I honestly hadn't expected such an understanding response. That was a surprising lesson to learn: someone in authority felt that my feelings and experiences were valid, and I was worth defending.

Early on at the NBA, I received a wise piece of advice from Ken. There were events that certain staff, including me, had to attend in order to assist. At those events, alcohol was prevalent, and we were supposed to participate. Although I was unaware of my predisposition for alcoholism at the time, I knew I had a tendency to drink an unnecessary amount and was concerned that things might go south at a work event. He advised me to mingle and look like I was joining in by ordering a club soda with lime. That way, others would assume I was drinking an alcoholic beverage with gin or vodka, but I wouldn't risk getting drunk and embarrassing the NBA. It was great advice, and I wish I could say I followed it beyond the NBA social gatherings. But alas, alcoholism is in my DNA, and I did succumb for many years.

It was at the NBA, during the holiday season, that I first encountered my creative gene. Part of my job was to put up and decorate the Christmas tree located in the reception area. I enjoyed the process of putting up the tree, especially since I could do it the way I wanted. After it was complete, as I was sitting at my desk, I realized the tree was really boring. Just a lot of silver, blue, and red balls. No character, at least in my opinion. This was the office of the commissioner of the National Basketball Association! We needed a more sports-oriented tree.

I contacted the marketing department and asked for two color sheets for each of the NBA teams. These sheets contained the logo and specific colors approved for use by each of the teams.

I cut out each of the logos and team names and taped them to the boring balls on the tree—with the NBA logo as the "star." Now that was a basketball tree! I had no idea how my boss would respond (or the commissioner, for that matter). Needless to say, the tree was a hit with everyone. I received lots of congratulations for taking the initiative. (Now you can buy ornaments for each of the teams—but mine was the first.)

Soon after that, an opportunity presented itself to move from the reception area into the inner workings of the league office as an assistant. I went for it. Knowing shorthand was a real plus, and I moved into the position of assistant to the director of media information.

Because of my position as assistant to the director of media information, I had direct contact with all the NBA teams as well as media outlets. I was happy with my job and my life. I still lived at home and paid rent, took the bus to the subway and then walked to the office, and I was paid a decent salary. However, it came to my attention from a colleague at the New Jersey Nets (now the Brooklyn Nets) that a higher-level position had opened up there. Another opportunity was about to present itself.

After driving to New Jersey for the interview, I learned that I would be administrative assistant to the general manager and the chief executive officer. Not one boss with two titles, but two different bosses. That had the potential of getting complicated, but I knew I was qualified for the position. I also realized that if I got the job, I would definitely have to move out on my own. My first apartment and the first female in my family to move out without getting married first!

This job change would give me the opportunity to remove myself from living with my parents, both of whom smoked like chimneys. And it would remove me from having to deal with (or in our case, not dealing with) the fact that Mom was drinking a lot. Her drinking was certainly the proverbial elephant in the room. Most evenings it was not possible to have an intelligent conversation with her. I would get home from work, grab something to eat, and go to my room. I considered marking the liquor bottles to see how much was gone from day to day. Little did I realize that if she was sipping on vodka most of the day, it meant there had to be a secret stash somewhere in the house. Unfortunately, I could never talk to my dad about the situation—in our home, females had no pertinent opinions.

The possibility of this job occurred at an important time in my life in other ways too. Since I was not dating anyone at the time, and my "long-distance relationship" seemed to be fading away, I was free to hightail it to another state and begin again. How exciting that I trusted my instincts and took the job! I threw a bunch of clothes into my car and headed out to New Jersey.

I moved in with the colleague who had recommended me for the job and lived with her for a short time until I could find an affordable apartment. I found one as quickly as I could since my clothes had to be stored in the closet with her cat's litter box. Not a great odor to wear to work each day!

Since I was the first of my group of high school friends to get my own place, I was excited to invite them over to my apartment for dinner. The response I got was, "You want us to drive to New Jersey? That's way too far!" Of course, what I heard was: "You want us to drive all the way to New Jersey to see you? You're not worth it." They never did come to visit. Not one of them. I was truly on my own. I had chosen to move out of state, away from my family, but I hadn't expected that I would permanently leave behind all friendships.

Working for a professional sports team is not as glamorous as one might think. Especially when you had to work games even on holidays. I missed a few Thanksgiving dinners because of home games.

The Nets headquarters was a typical office environment, complete with office politics. Additionally, my position required a challenging and delicate balancing act to meet the needs of both top executives of the team. It was especially dicey when they both called me in for dictation at the same time. On one occasion, I stood back and said, "You guys decide ... because even though I'm good, I certainly can't take shorthand from both of you at the same time."

One particular memory stands out while I was working at a Nets game against the San Diego Clippers. The Clippers had one of the first team mascots—the "San Diego Chicken," which actually was a young guy in a chicken suit. Before the game started, I noticed the "Chicken" interacting with our team cheerleaders. He was grabbing them (inappropriately, in my opinion), and they would turn red, giggle, and try to move away. As I walked past him to deliver some information to the courtside officials' desk, he grabbed me by the arm, apparently expecting me to react like the cheerleaders. Instead, I smiled at him (you never knew when TV cameras were on) and said, without changing my expression, "If you even think about touching me again, I will rip that chicken head off and punch your lights out. And leave the girls alone, too, because I am watching you."

The San Diego Chicken experience provided me the opportunity to speak my truth and not compromise my values or undervalue my own strength and worth. Just because some creep was in a mascot costume did not give him any right to inappropriately touch anyone—male or female. But it did give him anonymity. And I stripped that away from him and called him out—all five feet four inches of me!

Unfortunately, while working for the Nets, alcohol began to set up house in my day-to-day activities. I had moved to a new state (a pattern that would continue for many years) and had no friends to hang out with other than work colleagues. When I did go out—which was rare because I experienced severe unease and anxiety in group situations—it was usually dinner and drinking. There was also no worse feeling than experiencing a sense of loneliness in a group of people. Drinks lessoned all of those feelings.

While I never drank at work or at lunch, I did start drinking as soon as I got back to my quiet apartment. I would drive back to my place after work and have at least five hours of nothing to do except care for my wonderful dog, Brandy. (Writing this, I just realized her name was alcohol-related. Ha!) Every evening, drinking became a habit to combat the long hours of aloneness. It would be almost fifteen years before I realized that alcohol was not and could not continue to be my companion.

CHAPTER 5

From Sports to Law

Don't put too much value on what others think.
Believe in yourself and you will succeed.

AFTER SEVEN YEARS OF WORKING for professional sports, a former colleague who I had worked with closely at the NBA contacted me and talked me into interviewing at a highly respected New York law firm. She shared with me that working for a lawyer would not only increase my career potential and expand my knowledge; it would greatly add prestige to my resume. This firm was one of the venerable New York firms whose place at the pinnacle of the law profession was unassailable, and for a new lawyer, this was the first step to the golden ring of partnership and, with it, lifetime tenure, prestige, and affluence.

I took a day off and boarded the train from New Jersey, traveling under the Hudson River to the World Trade Center. Then it was a subway ride to their midtown offices. The offices were five full floors in the McGraw-Hill Building on Sixth Avenue (also known as Avenue of the Americas, which is never used by a true New Yorker). I met with the head of the human resources department, and after a short interview, which included showing off my shorthand and typing skills, she immediately took me to meet with the lead attorney of the trusts and estates department. He was thrilled that I took shorthand, and because of that skill, he was inclined to overlook the fact that I had no legal background. He said I could easily learn all I needed to know about trusts and estates to be successful in the position. I was offered the position on the spot, and I immediately said yes.

Since I was living in New Jersey at the time, my new daily commute included the train to New York, the subway to get closer to my office building, and then a walk to our offices. I was definitely one of the "working girls," dressed in a professional suit, stockings, and sneakers until I got to my desk. I kept a drawer full of dress shoes and would change into the ones best suited for my outfit for the day, then remembered to change back to sneakers before I left work.

The law firm was the epitome of an "old boys' club," with its dark wood paneling, massive full-floor library, and marble stairs in the reception area. The firm had five floors, the elevators were slow, and I took the stairs whenever possible.

Working in the trusts and estates department was challenging—and it was boring. When I tell you this was a boring area of law, for me it was actually *the most boring* of the boring areas of law practice. Besides that, my boss was overweight and battled diabetes. Health-wise, he was not doing well. It was not uncommon for me to come into the office in the morning before he arrived to clean up the empty martini glasses and debris left over from the night before. I'm glad it didn't start until after I went home for the day.

He finally decided to attend a health and wellness program at Duke University in North Carolina and would be gone from the firm for at least three months. As an assistant whose boss is on vacation, or in my case, on sabbatical, you don't just sit in the empty office and file papers. No, you bounce around and fill in for any lawyer whose assistant is out sick or on vacation. During those months, I got a crash course in almost every department in the firm.

On one occasion when I was temping in the litigation department, all the assistants were in a twitter because Superman was coming in for a deposition. Yes, Christopher Reeve was going to be in the building, and the girls were all excited. We received notice that *no one* was to hang around the conference room where the deposition was being held, and *no one* could be on that floor unless your office was there. It just so happened that I had to deliver papers to someone on that floor. I knew I had to be quick and stealthy, so I hightailed it down two flights of stairs, swung open the door, ran around the corner, made the turn, and ... smashed right into Superman!

Boy, were we both surprised. And holy crap, was he solid. I bounced off him and nearly hit the floor. Mr. Reeve did not move. We both apologized to each other. He even made sure I wasn't hurt. I could see our lawyers watching me. I said thank you to Mr. Reeve, wished him luck with the deposition, and went on my way. The look on the lawyers' faces was priceless. They had definitely expected me to get all giggly and probably wet myself. They forgot that I came from a professional sports background, and "celebrity status" did not impress me. After all, everyone puts their pants on one leg at a time. I was a professional legal assistant and damn good at my job, no matter who I inadvertently slammed into.

One of the other attorneys I temped for was female. On my very first day temping for her, she came back from lunch and asked if I had finished a project she had given me earlier to complete. Since I was not well-versed in her legal domain, it was taking me longer than she thought appropriate. She said to me, "Don't worry, dear, I'm sure you are doing your level best." I looked at her as if to say, "You didn't just say that to me, did you?" Although I didn't come right out and speak what I was thinking, I'm sure my eyes and mouth were wide open. She smiled and walked into her office.

I continued to process the putdown. *How rude! And to another woman! Nice way to support and make your staff feel empowered and an important part of the team.* I was helping her out, for Chrissakes! I learned a valuable lesson at this early stage of my professional career: Never treat your staff as inferiors because you seriously and literally cannot do it without them. I took this to heart, and it is still one of my important values. Luckily, I only had to fill in for her assistant for the rest of that day and was reassigned to another lawyer for the rest of that week.

After three months of filling in for vacationing or out-sick assistants and learning quite a bit about different areas of law, I found out that my boss would be staying at Duke University for another three months. It was time for the firm to find me something more permanent. I ended up in corporate law—not as boring as trusts and estates. I was relatively happy working for a new lawyer, and it gave me the opportunity to expand my knowledge in another area of law practice, which only added to and strengthened my resume.

Not long after starting with him, I was approached by human resources and encouraged to consider interviewing for the position of legal assistant to the chairman of the litigation department. After doing a quick research check, I was slightly impressed by his current position and his past accomplishments and, yes, just a bit intimidated. I had learned that he had been an assistant attorney general in charge of the Antitrust Division at the US Department of Justice, where he had been responsible for the development and enforcement of antitrust policy for the US.

I knew nothing about litigation. I did know from my temporary adventures that it was certainly more exciting than anything else I had experienced. I also knew I could learn, so as I usually do when an opportunity lands in my lap, I responded, "Sure, why not?" In other words, I felt the fear of my perceived limitations and leaned into it.

My interview seemed to go well. I knew he was interviewing others who most likely were more qualified, but after about a week, I was offered the job. I found out later that HR pretty much had to talk each of us into working with the other. I wasn't sure about litigation, and he didn't want to steal another lawyer's assistant. One of the key factors was that I was one of only a handful of assistants who still took shorthand, which apparently sealed the deal.

Working for the head of litigation was a steep learning curve. Litigation is highly complex, so I had a lot to learn—and I enjoyed every minute of it. We did have to get to know each other, and he quickly found out I could speak my mind and be a little feisty too.

On one occasion, early in our working relationship (about two weeks in), he called me into his office and asked me to get a certain gentleman on the phone. I went back to my desk and looked on the Rolodex (yes, the big wheel with all the individually typed cards on it) but did not find the man's name and phone number. Being the head of the department, we had some new technology as well, which included a digital Rolodex on my computer that also automatically dialed the number. Again, no listing. I then went into his office and said, "I'm sorry, but I cannot find his phone number. Please tell me what firm or company he is with, and I'll get him that way."

He was clearly annoyed and not at all happy. After harrumphing, he answered, "Terri, did you see a listing for a man named Harold, with the same last name?"

"Yes, I did," I responded.

"Well, Joseph is his brother, and they're at the same number."

I gave a short pause, put my hands on my hips, and said, "Well how the hell am I supposed to know that?!"

He sat back in his chair while I wondered if I had just ended my short career in litigation. After a moment, he smiled and said, "You're right. Please get me Joseph on the phone."

I left the room and made the call. My new boss now had a glimpse into my character and personality.

On another occasion, he came to realize this aspect of my character was not going to go away. One of his major clients was in for a meeting, as we were scheduled to go to trial shortly. Whenever this client came in for a meeting, I was required to stop on my way into work and pick up a bag of regular M&M's. Making sure our client, the executive vice president and chief operating officer of his company, had M&M's was not particularly onerous. This time, however, I purchased peanut M&M's. As he was leaving following their pretrial meeting, he said to me, "Terri, do you get the M&M's?" I shook my head yes. I could see my boss behind our client putting his hand to his head, like, "Oh no, here we go."

The client continued, "You know I prefer the regular M&M's."

To which I responded, "Well, I do now, but since I buy the candy, and since I pay for them, I thought a change might be nice."

He laughed heartily, handed me a twenty-dollar bill, and said, "Fair enough. Here's for next time ... the ones I like."

I smiled and responded, "Of course."

My boss would see my feistiness more than a few times while we were at the firm as well as when we moved to another company together. He later told me that it was a character trait he grew to secretly admire throughout our many years together.

Something I learned about myself early on was that I am not easily intimidated. I do not back down. And I don't care what your title is. However, I did understand how to play the game. I knew when to call my boss by his last name and when his first name was appropriate. And I knew how to treat clients and how to take care of them. All the while being true to my values.

One of the many things I was responsible for was the monthly billing reports that we sent out to clients. Most were standard and needed no changes. One client, however, refused to pay for "secretarial time." In a law firm, it's all about billable hours. You make copies, you use a client number. You break down your administrative time (including preparing their bills) into client numbers. For this one client, I had to get creative and come up with a plan. I took all the administrative time billed, removed it from that line item, and added it into other line items so that it totaled the same amount. The client still paid for administrative fees, but I just called it something else. One of my many strong suits that came into sharper focus: Think outside the box and color outside the lines. Life is much more interesting and fun that way.

It was early 1991. A typical day at the office. Little did I know that this day was going to lead to an opportunity for me to make a truly life-changing decision. One of our major clients was The Walt Disney Company. My boss was the company's main outside counsel for all substantial litigation requirements. He had been on the phone frequently over the prior week with the president of The Walt Disney Company, Frank Wells. This was unusual because, as far as I knew, we did not have any active litigation cases going on with Disney. He asked me to make travel arrangements for him to fly to California to meet with Disney executives. Not too unusual, but I knew something was definitely going on.

The day after he returned from California, he called me into his office and asked me to close the door. A warning sign, if ever there was one. He proceeded to tell me that he had been offered a position at The Walt Disney Company. It required moving to Los Angeles. He let that sink in. My first thought was, *Here I go again ... looking for another lawyer to work for. And I really like the relationship I've built with him. Damn.*

Instead, he continued, "What I need to know is this: Are you part of my relocation package?" I wasn't sure I knew what that meant. The confusion on my face must have triggered something because he then said, "Take a few days to think about it." At that moment, I realized he was asking me to go with him to work at Disney. *The opportunity to move to California and get to work at Disney, a company I've revered since I was a little girl? I would be working for Mickey Mouse, and I would probably meet Peter Pan and Tinker Bell too.* I took a breath and said, "Of course. Yes!" He told me to check with my boyfriend and my family and let him know in the morning. I responded, "I'll check with them, but the answer is still absolutely *yes!*" There was no way I would let this opportunity pass me by.

I did talk it over with my boyfriend, Peter, and he told me that he was not ready to make a commitment, and under the circumstances, he could not ask me to stay. It was an amazing opportunity, and he knew I could not pass it up. But if things didn't work out, I could always come back.

In any corporation, situations do not stay quiet. In my case, before the end of the week, many of my coworkers began to ask me about going to Disney and expressed how unusual it was for a boss to take his assistant with him. They also told me that they had heard I would be making a six-figure salary. I mentioned this to my boss and laughingly asked if I could confirm the number. He sort of smirked at me and shook his head no. (While I did not start out at six figures, I did end up there.)

Just before we left, the firm had a going-away cocktail reception for their lead litigator: my boss. He insisted that I be invited too. Many companies, and especially a law firm, were extremely class conscious, and most of the time, classes did not mix. Insisting that I be included in the going-away celebration was a first for the firm, and I hope it was not the last. I thoroughly enjoyed the feeling of being included, as I hadn't experienced this often. It was one of those times when he made sure I was a part of what was happening, when he indicated that we were a team. If only it had lasted.

A funny thing I found while packing was a rejection letter from The Walt Disney Company dated right after my graduation from high school. At the time, I had written to Disney inquiring about an entry-level secretarial job, and they very nicely turned me down. Now, a few years later, they were paying for me to relocate to Los Angeles and work as the administrative assistant to an officer of the company. What an incredible turn of events!

A few weeks after agreeing to move cross-country, a moving van pulled up and movers packed up my apartment. Then a flat-bed truck arrived and hauled off my car. In the next blink of an eye, I found myself sitting in Newark Airport with a one-way ticket to Los Angeles. An exciting new adventure. Another opportunity to begin again. Was I flying toward my future? Or was I running from my past? One way or the other, I knew this experience was going to be an amazing and perhaps somewhat overwhelming opportunity. I was ready for the task, though, excited and delighted for this new and unchartered adventure.

This would be the second time I took advantage of exploring an unknown opportunity and moving out of state to start over. I didn't know if my long-distance relationship would work out (the last one hadn't), but I did know that I would see Peter at least once more. He was caring for my dog, Maxx, and would be flying out to California with Maxx as soon as I was settled.

CHAPTER 6

The Adventure Begins

What dreams await at the top of the castle?

LOS ANGELES INTERNATIONAL AIRPORT (LAX). Chaos central. Especially for me, traveling alone, both nervous and excited to be on my own in a new city and a new state. I was not a comfortable traveler, so navigating my way through a huge airport like LAX in an attempt to get from the arrival gate to baggage claim was my first California challenge.

After retrieving my bags, it was off to locate the rental car agency to acquire my rental car. Once that was done, I had to figure out how to get out of the airport and on to the freeway. I am directionally challenged on a good day, and this *adventure* tested my ability to trust in myself and accept whatever obstacles came my way.

I had printed out a copy of directions from LAX to The Walt Disney Company in Burbank, plus another set of directions from Burbank to my new apartment, which was luckily only a few minutes' drive from the Disney offices. Because I had been taking the bus-train-subway to the law firm for a few years, I was not used to doing so much high-stress driving. Especially in a totally new and unfamiliar environment. It was challenging to read driving directions while navigating the absurd LA traffic and trying not to get killed before I even started my dream job.

My first "WTF moment" was driving on Sepulveda Boulevard as I attempted to get out of the airport. All of a sudden, right in front of me, a freakin' 747 crossed the road. I nearly stood the car on its front end as I slammed on the brakes and slowed down to try and figure out why a plane had just crossed over. I looked around and saw that everyone else was driving normally (well, normally for LA drivers). After my heart rate and breathing slowed, I realized it was an optical illusion—the road I was traveling on dipped under an overpass that was an active runway entrance road for departing flights. Welcome to LaLa Land. The land of illusion.

I drove directly to the Disney Studio lot, gave my name at the security gate, stuck on my visitor pass, and drove in, passing under the iconic gateway. *Oh my gosh! I'm really here and they are letting me in!*

As I drove past security to enter the underground parking, there it was off to my right, another iconic symbol: the dwarf building. This building, where I would work for the next twelve years, was called the dwarf building because the roof was held up by all seven dwarfs. Back in the day (1937, actually), if it had not been for the success of *Snow White*, there never would have been the financial stability necessary to become the global behemoth known as The Walt Disney Company. The front of the Team Disney building was a nod to that fact: the dwarfs hold up the roof of the corporate offices.

The building was officially named Team Disney Burbank Building, and in 2006, it was rechristened to Team Disney—The Michael D. Eisner Building.

By this time in my life, a pattern had firmly developed. When an opportunity presented itself, I went for it—most of the time, with no real planning. More like an "I'll figure it out as I go along" kind of plan. In this case, however, I did do some planning ahead of time. Knowing I would be totally on my own—not knowing anyone, or where to shop, or even how to get from one place to another—I had given some thought to how I would manage during the first few days on my own. I patted myself on the back for having had the wherewithal to mail myself a care package in advance of my arrival. I sent the package to the manager of the Disney Legal Department. Because of my prior duty at the law firm handling client litigation billing, Diane was the only person I had a relationship with at Disney before arriving in California.

I found my way to her office on the third floor, and we finally met for the first time. She showed me around a bit and then presented me with my first Disney Cast Member nametag. Talk about feeling the pixie dust all around me. We then took the elevator up to the sixth floor—the top of the castle.

I would find out later that there had been much discussion as to where my boss's office was going to be. It was quite a coup for us to land on the sixth floor. The only other executives on that floor were The Walt Disney Company CEO, Michael Eisner; president Frank Wells; the president of Walt Disney Studios, Jeffrey Katzenberg... and now us! Diane and I didn't stay long since I technically wasn't supposed to start work until the following day. We went back down to Diane's office, and I took my care package from her and headed off to find a store and then my new apartment.

That first night, I was grateful that I had sent myself some important and much-needed items, since all my belongings would not be arriving for another few days. I'd included an air mattress, towels, a lamp, and a plug-into-the-wall landline phone (the personal cell phone was not yet ubiquitous). On my way to my new apartment, I had stopped to pick up some food, and for my first California meal, I prepared a Swanson fried chicken TV dinner. I know, talk about living on the edge.

After cooking the dinner, I pulled it out of the oven with one of the towels I'd packed for bathing and sat down to eat. It was then that I realized I had not packed any utensils. The fried chicken was easy to pick up, but what was I going to do about the corn and mashed potatoes? After laughing at myself and knowing no one was watching, I scooped up the potatoes with two fingers, smashed them into the corn, and voila! Corn-taters! I truly enjoyed my first meal in my California apartment.

The next day began my tenure at The Mouse House. I was beyond excited to drive up to the gate, give my name, and get waved through. From the beginning, I knew that being able to park in the cast member underground parking structure on the executive level was a perk—one of the many that came with working on the top floor of the castle. I got on the elevator and made my way up to the sixth floor, introduced myself to the security guard and went into my office. As I sat down behind my desk, I reveled in the realization that I was now an official Cast Member of The Walt Disney Company.

My boss would not be arriving for another week, so I was literally on my own initially. He had told me to learn everything

I could and get him set up so he could hit the ground running when he arrived. As I explored my new office surroundings, I was surprised to find that all my file cabinets were empty. Since I had never started a position literally from scratch before, it was exhilarating that I was being given the opportunity to blaze my own trail and set up a filing system that made complete sense to me. But I did think it was odd that the individual who'd held the position previously did not provide us with any legal files. Apparently, he kept all the files with him when he and his assistant moved over to a new position within the company.

That first day, I got my Disney ID card, my car access sticker, my official lanyard to display my employee ID, found my way to the commissary, and yes, even acquired my first pair of Mickey Ears. I loved being able to walk down Mickey Avenue and see all the places where Walt Disney himself had walked and brought the magic to life. I was thrilled to learn about the history of the Disney campus and have the opportunity to walk through the underground tunnels between the Ink and Paint building and the Animation building. These tunnels had been added when the animators realized that they could not take the chance of rain getting on the cels, the transparent celluloid sheets used in all the original animation movies and cartoons before they made it to the multiplane camera (which Walt Disney had invented to provide the depth of scene he needed in the animated movies) for production. Now, I was a part of the magic. Once again, the learning curve would be straight up, but I knew I would love every minute of it.

Our offices were on a working studio lot, which meant you never knew who you might see on your way to pick up lunch. A gladiator? A knight or lady-in-waiting? Not too long after my boss arrived, as I was coming back with my lunch (I always ate at my desk), I encountered actor Kevin Costner walking toward me. This was at the height of his career, just after the release of *Dances with Wolves*. He saw me approaching, and I could see him brace for the fangirl reaction. What I did was smile at him and say, "Hello, I appreciate your work." Then I kept walking.

He was visibly relieved and appreciative. When I got back to my desk, I walked into my boss's office and said, "I just passed Kevin Costner downstairs. I've decided we can stay, so I'm going to finish unpacking now."

Disney's president, Frank Wells, came across as a gruff, serious man, and I witnessed executives cower in his presence. There were times when I was on the elevator with him and watched as someone else got on but didn't push the button for their floor. Apparently, they didn't want to make him have to wait for them to get off. I think he enjoyed seeing if he could knock someone off their game.

My boss's office had originally been an empty office just across an open area from Frank Wells's office. Off to one end of the open area was a small conference room, usually used by him and other high-level executives. I was the nearest assistant to the conference room, and he frequently held meetings there. One time, he yelled, "Terri!" so loudly that I walked over to the conference room, stood in the doorway, and yelled back, "What, Frank?!" The meeting attendees looked at me in horror. From their wide-eyed expressions, I knew they were thinking: "Well, there goes her job!"

Frank had his back to me. Slowly, he turned around, smiled at me, winked with a slight nod, and said, "Would you get 'so-and-so' on the phone?" I smiled back at him, and responded, "Of course, Frank. Do you want to take it here or in your office?" We were friends from that day forward.

It was the night of April 3, 1994. My boss called me at home. In and of itself, a very unusual occurrence. And in this case, a very sad one too. He telephoned to inform me that Frank Wells had been killed in a heli-skiing accident in the mountains of Nevada. We had no idea how this was going to affect us, but he wanted me to be ready when I went to work the following day.

Needless to say, everyone was walking around like zombies, and not much actual work got done that day or for a few days after. Since my office was right next door, and I knew that Frank's assistant would not be in that first day after the accident, I went into his office and sat for a while. I gave thanks for having had the opportunity to know and work with him and cried at his loss. Frank Wells had been a huge presence in the company.

Although everyone felt his loss, we and Disney would carry on. Within a few months of his death, necessary restructuring at the top began to take shape, and my boss was promoted. With that promotion, although he did not get the title of "president," we did get many of the responsibilities. And just before the end of the year, we finally were approved to move across the hall into Frank's empty office. This was quite the upgrade, especially for me. There was desk space for two assistants, although we did not use the other desk immediately, a private bathroom (for my boss, but of course I used it too), my own file room, and a glorious outdoor balcony.

After a few weeks of getting familiar with the increased amount of responsibilities, I walked into my boss's office and said that it was great he got a promotion, more money, and stock options, but ... what about me? His new position meant I had many more responsibilities and an increased workload too. He looked at me rather stunned, as I had never before asked for a new title or an increase in salary. He sat back in his chair and crossed his arms. I could see the wheels turning as he decided how to respond. He told me he could not pay me as much as CEO Michael Eisner's assistant was being paid. I responded, "That's not what I'm asking for," to which he asked, "So what are you asking for?"

I have no idea what made me say this, but my response was, "Well, what if I quit?"

"Wait, what?" Apparently, that got his attention.

"What if I quit? How much would it cost you to replace me?"

He frowned and said he would look into it. The next day, he told me I would be getting a significant increase, but no title change. I could certainly live with that. From that day forward, title or no title, I was the "chief of staff" to a high-ranking officer at The Walt Disney Company.

In addition to what is known as a Silver Pass, a special perk I was given because of who I worked for, I had the ability to get a special price for a room at Walt Disney World. I also had access to dinner reservations, personal behind-the-scenes tours, and even a walk-through of the maze of tunnels under the Magic Kingdom.

In December 1991, I arranged to meet my boyfriend, Peter, at WDW for our first vacation together since I had moved across the country. I had booked a room for us at The Grand Floridian. The Grand Floridian is the preeminent hotel on the Disney Florida property. It is a combination of Victorian elegance and modern sophistication.

When I checked in, I received fabulous service and was escorted to the honeymoon suite. My good friend and colleague, Rita, had arranged the upgrade. This was the same room that Michael Eisner stayed in when he was on property. It overlooked the lagoon where the nightly water parade was held. I was thrilled.

Peter and I had not seen each other since his visit in May, when he flew out to specially deliver my dog, Maxx, who he had cared for while I got settled. Our relationship had progressed, and he was planning to move to Los Angeles in January to join me on the West Coast. Peter arrived the day after I did, and I met him at the front of the Grand Floridian as he drove in. What I didn't know was that he was planning to propose while we were on vacation. Since he would be moving to join me in LA in January, I presumed we would get married. But I was unaware of his imminent plans.

He had already been in contact with my friend Rita, and everything was set. We went to dinner at Victoria & Albert's, and as the waiter removed the cloche from my dessert, there was a ring box perched on the plate. I opened the ring box and saw a ring covered in what looked like black wax. Trying not to look overly alarmed, I was thinking, *What is this? Why is there black wax all over my engagement ring?*

Peter saw my confused face, stood up, pulled another box out of his jacket pocket, and said, "You were supposed to get this," as he opened the box to reveal my beautiful diamond ring. He got down on one knee and proposed. Of course I said yes, and everyone in the dining room applauded. The ring in the ring box turned out to be a curved horseshoe nail. Peter said there was no way he was going to turn over the real ring to the Victoria & Albert's staff, and he knew he had to present something from under the dessert cloche. He had sent the ring box and horseshoe nail "ring" to Rita days earlier, and she had helped set up the grand proposal.

Dom Perignon was brought over, courtesy of WDW general counsel (Rita's boss) and his wife, and we toasted our engagement. When we arrived back at our room, there was another bottle of Dom Perignon. This time courtesy of my boss and his wife. We also had adorable strawberries dressed as tuxedoes sitting in Cinderella's glass slipper. I knew Disney did things above and beyond, but this time I was on the receiving end. I'd never had expensive, fancy champagne before, and now I had had two bottles in one night, plus strawberries in Cinderella's slipper. It seemed everyone had known about this proposal except me. Of course, being kept in the dark and yet being presented with such a grand evening of wonderful surprises was well worth having been "left out" of the planning for this spectacular moment in my life.

CHAPTER 7

Legal Mickey and the First Legal Retreat

Trust in yourself and be audacious.

ABOUT TWO YEARS INTO OUR ADVENTURE at Disney, my boss decided it would be a great idea to bring all the Disney lawyers together for a three-day retreat. It was my job to pull the whole thing together. Okay, well, this was a new addition to my responsibilities. Bringing together 250 lawyers from all over the world and providing multiple small-group activities throughout the weekend would be a huge undertaking, especially while continuing all of my normal daily responsibilities.

But, sure, easy-peasy, no problem. I got to work.

First thing we needed was a resort that could handle 250 rooms over three days. Basically, we were going to take over the entire property. I made the decision not to hold the event on Disney property, so that no one would have the excuse or distraction not to participate in our event activities. I told my boss that I needed to visit what I considered to be the best choice to make sure they could handle our group. I also wanted the opportunity to inspect the property and negotiate terms. He said I could go, but it had to be on a weekend. If it couldn't be done on a weekend, then Diane, the corporate legal department manager, would need to go instead. *Really?* I found it hard to believe he couldn't get along without me for one day, but rather than protest, I did what I had to do to ensure I could oversee this event from the beginning: I went on a Saturday.

After securing the resort—Rancho Bernardo in San Diego—I immediately put together a team to assist with all the necessary details. My first appointment was Diane. I knew she would have the necessary skills to be my best second-in-command. And since she had been the first one to welcome me to the Disney family when I first arrived, we had developed a special relationship. I knew I could depend on her to have my back if necessary. I also knew there was no way I could coordinate the travel, arrival, and needs of each lawyer without her expertise and knowledge. Plus, she would be able to help keep me stable and grounded as the craziness increased.

I also requested that the assistant to the general counsel of Walt Disney World be required to come, as she knew and could corral all of the WDW lawyers. One less possible headache for me. Additionally, I required that another top assistant accompany us to be in charge of our onsite business office. Because there is never an "off" day at Disney legal, I had to assume that almost all 250 attorneys would be continuing to work. We were going to need twelve fax machines and all the paper necessary to keep them humming, as well as multiple phone lines and available workspace.

This was the first time I was presented the opportunity to facilitate, coordinate, and actually build from scratch a Disney legal event. The best part of all was that I had no budget! That certainly made things a whole lot easier. It was also the first time something like this had been done in the legal department, so I was able to set my own bar. And, yes, I set it high. This was Disney, after all, and we do things *"to infinity and beyond"*!

In addition to all the details and coordination, I decided that, of course, we needed to give away a goody bag to each attendee. I called the heads of every department (Consumer Products, Hyperion Books, Walt Disney Studios, Disneyland, Disney World, Imagineering) and asked them to donate three hundred of whatever item they had stored in a closet. While putting that all together, I realized I would need something to put everything in. I asked consumer products to recommend a reputable vendor for a custom duffel bag.

It was then I noticed that many other departments had their own version of Mickey Mouse. I decided that legal needed its own Mickey too—"Legal Mickey." I worked closely with the designers in Consumer Products and gave them a few parameters to start from. Mickey needed to be wearing judge's robes, while holding the scales of justice and a law book. Each time I was sent a new rendition, I made a tweak or two. However, after more than a few passes back and forth, something was still not quite right. Then it hit me. All the lawyers in the motion picture division came to work every day in casual wear. I wanted to make sure I included them, so under Mickey's judge's robes we added a pair of red sneakers. Perfect.

During the event, everyone gathered together each evening for a "formal" dinner. While setting up in the main ballroom the first afternoon, I was asked by the resort staff if I wanted a table for my staff and me set up in the kitchen or off to the side out in the hallway. Neither option was acceptable to me. As I had learned early on at my previous law firm about how not to treat your staff, I certainly wasn't going to have us sitting in another room like peons. I instructed the resort staff to set up a smaller table in the main ballroom off to the side but definitely part of the celebration activities. We were an integral part of this event, and I wanted to make sure my staff knew they were valued.

The retreat was a huge success, despite a few glitches. One in particular still makes me chuckle. After all the festivities were over on Friday night and the room was clearing out, I finally went back to my room. I was exhausted and done for the day. Just before midnight, I received a phone call from the night-duty resort manager. It seemed his staff had tried to close down the ballroom, but a few of my attorneys were still singing around the piano. In order to let the resort staff close the room, the attorneys rolled the piano out into the hallway to continue their merriment. An inappropriate "solution." The night manager asked me to come down and fix things.

I threw on a sweatshirt and pants and made my way back down to the ballroom. When they saw me coming and saw the look on my face, they were quick to invite me to join the revelry.

"Put the piano back," were the first words out of my mouth.

"But we're still singing."

"Put the piano back."

"But it's on wheels and we're not in the way."

"Let me explain what happens here. The hotel cannot leave

you alone with the piano that belongs in the ballroom, and if anyone stays with you, I get charged triple overtime per hour. When your boss asks what the additional charge was for, I will tell him. So ... put ... the ... piano ... back."

They got the message, rolled the piano back into the ballroom, and went their separate ways. I don't want to know what else might have happened that night if they hadn't complied with my request, and since I did not get any further late-night calls, I'm pretty sure everyone was on their best behavior for the rest of the weekend.

What I tell people about that three-day event is this: "Imagine putting on a three-day wedding for 250 brides. That is what it's like dealing with 250 attorneys for three days." Being given the opportunity to establish a successful Disney Legal Department retreat for the first time from the bottom up was one of the most appreciated feathers in my mouse ears. I'd been given carte blanche, and I was able not only to utilize my strengths and creativity, but I was given the freedom to discover the skills and talents I didn't know I had as an event coordinator and leader of a fabulous team who I knew were with me every step of the way. I depended on them to do all they could to make this an amazing and successful event, and it was.

As a team leader, I handled every behind-the-scenes "glitch," and not one attorney, including my boss, ever knew that anything went wrong. As far as they were concerned, everything went smoothly and successfully. Everyone had a great experience, especially enjoying the opportunity to finally meet people they had only previously worked with by phone. They were able to confer with fellow experts face-to-face to help out with challenging legal issues.

For me, it was one of the most rewarding experiences I had at Disney, and knowing I pulled it off still makes me smile. At the final dinner, my boss called me up to the front of the room and shared with me and the attorneys how proud and appreciative he was to me and my team for pulling off a spectacular weekend retreat. As I stood next to him in front of the room full of Disney legal executives, he showered me with praise and appreciation. Hearing out loud that he'd had the trust, faith (with a little bit of pixie dust), and the unwavering pride and conviction in me that I would pull off this fabulous, successful, and historic Legal Department event was the validation and appreciation I craved. I was embarrassed to be in front of the crowd, and yet for the first time in my life, I received the appreciation and recognition of my skills and value that I so deeply longed for. It was also the first time I had ever received a standing ovation, and it felt wildly fulfilling.

The Disney Legal Department Retreat continued to be held bi-annually for the remainder of my time with the company. And with each passing year, the events got better and better.

CHAPTER 8

Vodka Bottles

Grief and loss don't need to be drowned in alcohol.

WORKING AT DISNEY UP TO THIS POINT, I never gave any thought to how much time I spent alone. I was a "one-person assisting staff," as we had not hired anyone to help me. Once a year, I was taken out to lunch by the vice president of Disney University, and my boss took me to the Rotunda, the executive dining room, every so often. Other than that, I lived at my desk.

After completing my usual ten-hour day, I went home, and the first thing I did was take a few swigs from the bottle of vodka I had hidden in a purse at the bottom of my clothes closet. By this time, it was more of a "habit," and different from what I'd done while living in New Jersey to make the long nights alone go by faster. Although I was now happily married, and Peter was a wonderful husband and companion, drinking had become something I was used to doing at the end of each day. And, apparently, it was something I was predisposed to since alcoholism runs in my family.

In July 1994, I received a call from my sister, Claudia, saying Mom had collapsed in a store and was in the hospital. My first question was, "Do I need to get on a plane?" "No," came the reply. "If she sees you, she might think things are really bad. Let's wait until we get more information."

Apparently, she had been food shopping and collapsed in the store. They called 9-1-1 and Mom was immediately taken to the hospital. My dad and Claudia were with her and gave me periodic updates by phone. The next day as I walked past security, Tom told me my sister had called. *Oh dear, this can't be good.*

I rushed to my desk and called her. Mom had had a bad night and was now on a respirator. Things did not look too good, she informed me, and I needed to get on a plane. I told my boss I would be leaving the following day and made arrangements for someone to cover my desk. I had no idea how long I would be gone.

Peter and I flew out as fast as we could. As we packed, I saw him look in the closet and hesitate. "Yes," I said, "bring a suit." We spent the next week back and forth between Dad's house and the hospital. My brother and his girlfriend at the time drove in from Massachusetts. We spent days at Mom's bedside without any conversations. She awoke every so often, but with the respirator in her throat, she could not speak. We took turns holding her hand, talking to her, and dabbing her dry lips with lemon balm. It was a long week.

At one point, the doctor arrived and asked us to come into the hallway. He told us Mom's kidneys were shutting down, and we would have to decide if we were going to put her on dialysis. Standing in the hallway as a family, we had to make a huge decision. If we agreed to dialysis, then it would be dialysis for the rest of her life. If we did not agree, then it could be fatal if her kidneys did not "kick in." Peter, bless his heart, was the only one of us who asked, "Would your mom want to have to go to a facility a couple times a week for dialysis?" It was extremely helpful to get a different yet pertinent perspective. We decided: no dialysis.

Early the next morning, we got a phone call to get to the hospital ASAP. We all threw on whatever clothes we could grab and hightailed it over. Mom had thrown a blood clot, which had caused a pulmonary embolism. We were all with her when she stopped breathing. She was only sixty-seven. Way too young, in my opinion, to leave this earth, but she also only weighed ninety-seven pounds.

I believe she had been slowly killing herself with too much alcohol and not enough food for quite some time. There were few, if any, deep or meaningful conversations about Mom's drinking over the years, but I was certain she'd never slowed down or stopped in the years since I lived at home. Her drinking was frequently the elephant in the room: we all knew—we just didn't discuss it often, or at all. As sad as it was, I was not surprised that we lost her so early in her life. We each said our goodbyes and left the room so Dad could have his time alone with her.

While my dad had taken on the chore of planning his own mother's and in-laws' funerals, my siblings and I had never before handled the many decisions a funeral entails. We knew Mom had requested cremation, and we all agreed to honor her request.

Off we went to the funeral parlor in Stroudsburg, Pennsylvania. The funeral director was respectful and attentive. We soon learned what we didn't know and, therefore, what questions we didn't even know to ask. After sharing that Mom would be cremated following the wake and Catholic Mass, he carefully suggested we might want to consider renting a casket. Who knew! Apparently, you can rent a nice casket for the services, and then, before cremation, the body is transferred into a plain wooden container. This seemed like a much less costly option—since the container would be burned, it would have been a terrible waste of a perfectly good, expensive casket. We agreed to that and picked out a lovely rental. Then we asked about picking out an urn for the cremains, and he gave us a small catalog. The funeral director also told us we could drive over to the crematorium, and they would probably have more urn options.

The next day, Claudia and I went off to the crematorium. My brother, Chris, had to drive back home to Massachusetts to get a suit. I'm guessing he'd been hopeful he would not need one when he originally packed to come. We drove into the cemetery and had to find our way to the crematorium. Not a building you want to be able to see from the road, it was way back in the far corner of the property. As we walked into the office area, my first thought was, *I've never seen such disorganization and stacks of paper in my life.* Someone came out from the back when they heard the door open and were very surprised to see us. "Hello, are you looking for the cemetery office?"

"No, we were referred by our funeral parlor that you might have more urn options to choose from. Our mom just passed, and we don't know how to go about this."

He casually mentioned that they didn't usually see people in their office but would look around in the back for an urn catalog. Since there was no place to sit, Claudia and I stood around and waited. After a short time, it got really warm in the office. Claudia was looking uncomfortable and commented on how hot it was. I made sure she wasn't kidding, and then I said, "Claudia, what did you expect? They're not baking cookies back there." I realized what I'd said, looked at her, and we both burst out laughing. Talk about a way to break the tension! I'm sure the gentleman trying to help us thought we had lost it because we were still laughing when he returned.

That evening, Dad was in the living room when I went to keep him company. "Did you see this?" he asked. It was Mom's death certificate. I looked at it, and under "cause of death," it stated "complications from alcoholism."

"Yes, I did," I responded.

"How could they put that on here?" he said and started to cry.

Everyone else in the family knew Mom drank a lot. We all knew that you did not call after four in the afternoon her time because you would not be able to have a coherent conversation with her. In this moment with Dad, it felt like a heavy responsibility to keep this knowledge to myself, knowing full well that I, too, had a drinking problem. It seemed the family patterns were firmly in place.

Claudia and I had spoken on occasion in the past of Mom's condition, usually when something occurred that we needed to share. Chris and I never spoke about Mom's behavior, and I never spoke about it to Dad either. This was not a time to change my response. As far as his comment about Mom's death certificate, I did not respond. I let him hold on to his need to not believe Mom was an alcoholic.

I felt extremely sad and regretted the fact that I would never be able to talk to Mom again. But I was also pragmatic—it was my perception that she and I had not enjoyed a close, loving, and nurturing relationship anyway. Mom had not been the one I called first with good news or to help dry my tears. I'd learned that lesson many times over the years. I loved her, of course. She was my mom. And I knew she did the best she could with the tools she had been given during her own upbringing. It was time for me to make peace with our relationship.

A few months later, I returned to Pennsylvania to help Claudia clean out Mom's things. Almost everything was going to Goodwill. Dad said he could not help at all and was grateful that we were going to do it for him. As we started cleaning out the closet in the den, we pulled out all the purses at the bottom. We found at least six bottles of vodka—some opened, some not. Claudia squirrelled them out of the house and into her car. We decided not to share with Dad just how much Mom had been drinking.

For me, it was a whack-upside-the-head moment. *I hide my bottle in a purse in the bottom of my closet too. Granted, I only hide one bottle, but is this a precursor to where I am headed if I continue down this path?*

It was this realization, as well as admitting to myself that my drinking was actually a problem. I hid my "stash," I cycled among three different stores to replenish my supply (so no one would suspect), and I drank every day. This was not what normal social drinkers did.

That holiday season, I was blessed with a lifeline from an unexpected source. One day, Brian, who worked in the Rotunda (the Disney executive dining room), stopped by my office. As we were talking, he mentioned that the holidays were difficult for Kathy, the director of the Rotunda, since many executives gave wine as a gift. She was a recovering alcoholic, so wine was not a great gift for her to receive.

Although it didn't seem appropriate for him to have revealed this information to me, I felt I had just received my own Christmas gift. Early the next day, I went over to the Rotunda and asked Kathy if we could talk. I told her what I'd learned from Brian the previous day and asked her for help. She was pleased to be able to help me. She promised that no one would know, and she would take me to my first AA meeting. A savior dropped in my lap—and I had the good sense to accept it.

She came with me to several AA meetings. I went once a week (not the "attend a meeting every day" AA suggestion for people at the beginning of recovery). But I did go every week for more than a month and then had to miss a meeting because of travel. The following week as I walked into the room, I was greeted as if they had never seen me. "Welcome, is this your first meeting?" *Really? Am I invisible? What the heck!* After the many meetings I'd attended, I was surprised to be looked at as an outsider. I definitely felt excluded, and I realized I didn't really fit in.

AA is a valuable institution, but it is not for everyone. Many of the women in the group had been attending the meeting for decades, telling the same story over and over and over. During the time I attended, I found that surprising. *Why haven't they moved past this?* I wondered. I didn't want to exchange one crutch for another, and I really did want to move past my drinking. Which is exactly what I did ... on my own.

It turned out that AA was not the right place for me, and I've never looked back, nor have I ever been tempted to drink again. Whenever we go out, I have Peter taste my "virgin whatever" first, just to make sure there is no alcohol in it. I also never order anything prepared with wine or other spirits. I know the alcohol content is cooked out, but I don't even want to taste it. And I've been sober for more than twenty-five years now.

CHAPTER 9

Company Perks and Intrigue

No matter how difficult it seems, know when it's time to move on.

ONE OF THE PERKS OF BEING the administrative assistant, aka the chief of staff, for someone so high up in the company was the occasional trip on the corporate jet. Quite a different experience from flying commercial. I flew with my boss to WDW on several occasions. When it came to international flying, though, I flew commercial. For instance, when I flew to Paris to facilitate a special meeting for all our

European attorneys, it was commercial—but business class, not economy.

I had been working at Disney for a few years before I found out that many of my compatriots attended some of the special events, like new ride openings. My boss never mentioned that to me, and it never occurred to me to ask. Eventually, one special event caught my attention. At the end of February 1995, I received a phone call from the assistant to the president of Disneyland Resorts. She wanted to know how many tickets my boss wanted for the opening party of the new Indiana Jones ride to be held on March 3. After checking with him, I called the assistant back and said that he wanted enough for all of his kids and grandkids. Then, on a whim, I asked if I could attend. She said, "Sure, how many for you?" I told her I needed four. I invited Diane and her husband to go with me and Peter.

When I was at the event, of course I ran into my boss and his family. He was quite surprised to see me and asked, "What are you doing here?"

"I was invited," I replied and left it at that.

During the event, I saw many of the other assistants in attendance and wondered why he hadn't thought to include me from the beginning. Was it really just a matter of doing an end run around the boss and asking for myself?

From my upbringing and past experience, this was an area where I did not know what the "pay to get included" currency was. Although he'd gone to great lengths at the law firm to make sure I was included, he never seemed to make sure I was in his guest count at Disney. In this case, I'm glad I asked for myself and was rewarded with the enjoyment of a first-class private Disney event.

The event took place after Disneyland closed for the night. Guests were met at the entrance to the park and escorted to Adventureland, where they were then presented with event credentials and allowed access to all of Adventureland. It was a magical evening. We could go on the ride as many times as we wanted, and there was never a queue to wait in. Although I did get my pants scared off me, as on one run through the tunnels to board the ride, I came around a corner, and hidden in an alcove in the "rock" wall was one of the kids from the TV show *Tool Time*. He jumped out at me and, oh my goodness, I almost peed myself. Needless to say, he thought it was hilarious.

Based on my success with attending the Indiana Jones event, I wanted to attend Walt Disney World's 25th anniversary event. Since this would require a flight to Florida, as well as tickets and a pass to all the special events, I decided that rather than an end run, I'd approach my boss directly. I went into his office and said, "I have never asked you to attend anything, but I would really like to attend the 25th anniversary festivities. I know I'd need to work while there, but I'd really like to go." He was immediately noncommittal and changed the subject. He never responded. Never. And I did not go.

I later learned that I was the only assistant who did not go. Once again, excluded. *Damn!* From my perspective, it was another "you're not worth including" message written on my personal whiteboard. This message had been written over and over throughout my life.

It was possible that because I supported my boss at the highest levels within the company, he needed me in the LA office to run day-to-day activities and make sure the wheels didn't fall off the bus. Since he never said anything further or provided any explanation, though, I had no way of knowing. Deep inside, I hoped that had been his reason for not including me.

In August 1995, I was called into the office on a Sunday to type up a letter of intent. I knew there was talk that CEO Michael Eisner wanted to bring in the head of Creative Artist Agency, Michael Ovitz, as president. Ovitz had a Hollywood reputation, was good friends with Eisner, but had no experience running a global public company. I was on the phone with Ovitz's attorney, who was dictating the letter. He was talking at an exceptionally slow pace, and I kept telling him to speed up.

"Are you taking shorthand?" he asked.

"Yes I am. You can speak faster," I replied.

"No way! When we're done with this, do you want to come work for me?"

I graciously thanked him and turned down the offer.

After typing up the letter and making additional changes required by my boss, I brought it into his office. He was headed over to Eisner's house to meet with Eisner, Disney's CFO, and Ovitz to make the initial offer. Every fiber of my being told me this was going to be a fiasco and a challenging time for Disney. Michael Ovitz was Hollywood royalty. The company he founded, Creative Artists Agency (CAA), was a privately held corporation. He had no knowledge or background running a public company that was a global behemoth. I knew they were making a huge mistake, and I felt strongly that I needed to say something. I handed over the letter, and before I left his office, I said, "I am a Disney shareholder, and as a member of the board of directors, it is your fiduciary responsibility to make sure this does not happen. I cannot be the only one who thinks this is the worst move ever."

He stared back at me, and I knew he knew I was right. It turned out I was. Less than fifteen months later, Ovitz was gone, with a severance package worth $140 million in cash and stock options.

Years later, in a class action court case brought about by Disney shareholders, the court ruled in favor of Disney and the exorbitant payout. However, Chancellor Chandler did send a message to all corporate boards by stating in his ruling, "Disney board members fell significantly short of the best practices of ideal corporate governance."

Dealing with Michael Ovitz during his tenure was an opportunity for me to, once again, stick to my guns, speak up, and get feisty when I needed to. He had an imposing attitude, and my intuition alarms went off from the moment I met him. I figured he couldn't directly fire me since I was the assistant to someone who had equal clout in the executive hierarchy, and it was my responsibility to protect and fight for my boss and, more importantly, for what I felt was the good of the company.

Rumor had it that everyone on his staff was terrified of doing something wrong. He demanded his afternoon coffee be delivered at a specific temperature, on a specific coaster. I witnessed him being acerbic, rude, and downright mean. This temperament was not the norm at our level of executive authority. At least not one I had ever encountered before. Frank Wells notwithstanding. Frank's bark was worse than his bite, and we appreciated each other. Michael, on the other hand, was overly demanding, caustic, and haughty.

My favorite "encounter" with Michael was the time I literally got the opportunity to lock him out. He had this annoying habit of walking through my boss's office via his back door and then through mine to access the conference room. On this occasion, my boss was in a meeting with an outside attorney as well as a member of the board of directors. Ovitz just walked on through. It was definitely a power play and a show of disrespect. When the meeting was over, I walked in and asked, "Are you okay with Ovitz just walking through like that?" He told me he wasn't. I walked over to the back door and locked it. His eyebrows shot up, but he smiled. "There, at least now he has to knock."

I told Michael Eisner's assistant that the back door would now always be locked. I asked her to give me a heads up whenever Michael Eisner was headed over so I could unlock the door for him, as it opened up into Eisner's waiting area.

The next time Ovitz tried to use our offices as a thoroughfare, he found the back door locked. My boss heard him jiggle the handle but didn't get up to open the door. Ovitz walked around and came through my office.

"Did you know the back door is locked?"

I responded politely, "Really? I had no idea."

We looked at each other, but I did not flinch. He knew I had his number and was not going to let him get away with disrespecting my boss. This one sign of disrespect from Ovitz had been eliminated.

Years later, while reading an autobiography of one of the

Disney executives, I found out that Michael had been extremely pissed that he did not get my boss's office when he came to the company. It probably explained why he'd insisted on using his office as a thoroughfare ... until I locked the door.

On the morning of July 31, 1995, I was walking to the elevator when I ran into the senior vice president of corporate alliances. He asked if I was excited about the new acquisition. I knew we were in talks to acquire either CBS or ABC, and the last I heard, CBS was in the forefront.

I commented, "So we're getting CBS?"

"No," he replied, "ABC."

The following summer, Michael Eisner held a meeting of the heads of all of the telephone companies in Aspen, Colorado. I was at the front desk of the Hotel Jerome picking up a package for one of the executive vice presidents. As I turned around, a very good-looking gentleman stopped me and asked, "Do you work for John?"

"No, I'm just picking up something for him," I replied and then introduced myself and told him who I worked for.

He put out his hand to shake mine and said, "Hi, I'm Bob Iger."

Wow! A corporate executive saying the first hello. What a nice guy, I thought. I escorted Bob to the conference room where the meetings were being held and went about my chores. I am not surprised that Bob was named CEO when Michael stepped down in October 2005, and in 2019, Bob was announced as *Time Magazine's* Business Person of the Year.

As ABC acclimated into Disney, I observed something I thought was rather unusual. I noticed that the former ABC executives were slowly taking over the positions of long-term Disney executives. In January 2000, Bob Iger was named president and chief operating officer of The Walt Disney Company. Once again, my boss was passed over as president, and October of that year, he left Disney. He decided to return to private law practice.

It's curious that after including me in his original move to Disney and working together for over a decade, we did not have a meaningful conversation about the future and how I fit in with those plans. We never discussed it. I was working for him one day and the next day I wasn't.

With his departure, I chose to stay on at Disney rather than look for a new job. I was placed with one of the ABC executives, another who had moved into the top of the Disney castle to take over running the company. The transition was challenging for me. Although he was general counsel for ABC and deputy general counsel for Disney, I lost my office, my prestige, and my parking spot.

I stayed with him from October 2000 until October 2002, but immediately realized that I was certainly not going to be his "chief of staff." No, I was just an assistant. And I had to wrap my head around that realization quickly. It was back to typing, filing, setting meetings, and keeping my opinions and knowledge to myself. It had been apparent to me in my relationship with my former boss that no matter what was going on, I knew he still considered me integral to his operation and his success. That was not the case in this new working relationship. We were very different people and had a very different interpretation of the definition of administrative assistant.

A major aha moment happened on September 11, 2001. It was very early morning on the West Coast. I was up as usual and had turned on the TV to get the early local news. As the TV screen came on, I saw it: the north tower burning and reporters trying to make sense of what was going on. And then, at 6:03 a.m. California time, I watched as the second plane hit the south tower. *WTF! What is happening? What should I do?* I immediately called my boss at home. I knew the north tower housed radio and television transmission equipment.

"You need to turn on the TV," I said as he picked up the phone.

"I'm on my way to the gym, I'll see the news there," he casually replied.

"No, there's something going on. You really need to see this now."

"I'll see it at the gym," came his response.

I knew this was going to have a major impact on ABC broadcasting, but he was blowing me off. It told me that he did not give any value to my role in his office. I was attempting to give him a heads up on this monumental, historic event, and yet he obviously did not give any credence to what I was trying to tell him. This would have major repercussions on all ABC radio and television broadcasting ... and on our relationship as well.

While it didn't register at that moment, I knew that our relationship would never amount to what I had hoped it would. At 6:59 a.m., I watched as the south tower collapsed, and I fell to the floor and cried—for the World Trade Center disaster, the people involved, and for my limited time left at Disney.

I went in to work that day, and we scrambled to get approval to piggyback our broadcast signals off towers in New Jersey. We also went into lockdown protocol since there were rumors that major US companies might also be targeted. Concrete barriers were laid out in front of the entrance to the studio complex, and we all had to wear our ID badges at all times. I even took to riding to work with my teddy bear. If I was going down, I wanted to make sure I had something to hang on to. Teddy did not need his own badge. Yes, I asked.

Early the following morning, my phone rang. "Is this ABC News?" came the very British voice. The phones in my boss's former New York office had been forwarded to my desk.

"Actually, you've reached ABC in California. How can I help you?"

"Can you get a message to ABC News? I wanted to let you

all know that we Brits are with you and you have our sincere sympathies."

"Thank you so very much. I'll make sure the message gets to the appropriate person."

I was deeply moved and grateful for the honor to have received that call. I called Peter Jennings, sole anchor for *ABC World News Tonight*, and relayed the message.

That day during my lunch hour, I walked down to the Disney store and bought a bouquet of roses. Then I walked over to the flagpole where the flag was flying at half-mast and gently laid the flowers at the base. I stood there for a few minutes, said a prayer for the safety of our country, and went back to work. The next day, I saw that hundreds of flower bouquets had been laid at the base of the flagpole. I was glad I'd been the first one to pay my respects and that the observance was carried on by so many others.

CHAPTER 9

Back to a Cubicle

One step forward, three steps back. Seriously?

I STAYED AT DISNEY FOR ONE MORE YEAR, but I was just going through the motions each day. I think my boss and I both knew it. As I struggled with the thought of leaving Disney altogether, Bob Iger's assistant, Connie, announced she was leaving and Bob was looking for a new assistant. *Why not?* I thought. I contacted my good friend, Carol, and asked her about the position and whether I could get an interview with Bob. She told me I needed to ask Connie. I called Connie and asked about being considered to replace her. She told me that she was not handling the interview process, and I needed to ask Carol. *WTF?* After doing this back-and-forth phone calling a few times, I realized I was never going to get an interview with Bob.

As I considered what to do next, I came to a conclusion: they could double my salary, but I still would not be fulfilling my soul purpose, and I certainly was no longer happy. I didn't really know what my soul purpose was, but I did know it was not sitting at a desk typing up broadcasting contracts. As much as I thought I'd be in the Disney castle for the remainder of my working career, it was time to admit that there had to be something more I needed to do—something that would bring me joy and a sense that what I was doing mattered.

Sometime in August 2002, my former boss was back visiting the studio lot and invited me to lunch. It turned out to be fortuitous that we had lunch that day. He told me how terrible his new assistant was and that it was just not working out. He wanted to know if I would give any thought to coming back to work for him.

I was flattered and quietly euphoric that someone valued my knowledge and expertise—especially him, who I'd missed working with. I also thought that we'd always had a mutually respectful working relationship, and his desire to have me rejoin him validated my sentiments.

After making my decision, I gave two weeks' notice. At the end of the first week, I called human resources and asked why my boss was not interviewing anyone to replace me. They said he had not told them to start looking. By mid-second week, he finally saw someone. Apparently, I was easily replaceable, or so he must have thought. I never did train anyone.

Prior to my departure, it was required to have an "exit interview," and I was told what day and time to meet with someone from HR. I insisted I meet with the vice president of the department. Since I was a high-level assistant, I was going to meet with the head of the department, or I would meet with no one. My request was granted, and I met with Carol. Sadly, it felt as if she was just going through the motions. We had been friends for more than a decade, yet she was distant—it felt like she was just paying me "lip service." Yes, it certainly was time to leave the Mouse House and move on to infinity and beyond.

October 2002. I drove to downtown LA in horrendous traffic to the Los Angeles offices of the law firm my former boss and I had worked at previous to Disney. It took me an hour and a half in stop-and-go traffic (mostly stop). I would have to do this twice a day ... every day. *Yikes, what have I gotten myself into?* When I finally arrived, there was a parking structure below the building for me to enter. I didn't have an assigned spot, but thankfully I didn't have to pay for it either.

These were typical law offices, in the sense that attorneys had window offices and assistants were clustered in cubicles out in the hallway. I reminded myself that at least I had my own cubicle and did not have to share space—although this was certainly a major step down from my Disney accommodations. Was I having a drug-induced flashback to my original law firm days? Nope, suck it up, buttercup, and make the best of it.

The first few weeks were okay. Nothing special—getting used to being back in the trenches of a law firm. To entice me to come back to work for him, my boss had told me during our lunch that his current assistant was just not working out. She couldn't hold a candle to me, he'd said, and he really needed me back. However, after talking to some of the other assistants, I found out that his assistant was told I hated working for my new boss at Disney and insisted that my former boss take me back. Talk about throwing me under the bus before I even arrived. After hearing that and trying to set the record straight, or at least give my rendition of the event, I knew I would not be making friends easily.

I don't recall that we were working on any specific cases at the time. I understood that at this point, with his resume, he was supposed to woo the important clients, to be what is known in the legal world as a "rainmaker." I did start noticing a pattern where he would come in on Monday and leave Tuesday for our other office in New York. I was alone much of the time with not much to do. And I was getting concerned that I would be assigned to an associate lawyer, which is typical in a large firm when they discover that you have a lot of free time on your hands. Usually, you work for both a partner and an associate, who has much more of the actual grunt work to do.

Before I started back at the LA firm, I had told my boss that I would need a week off in November, as it was Peter and my tenth wedding anniversary, and we had already made plans. HR had approved my vacation time, and Peter and I were able to take our trip as planned. On the Monday I returned from vacation, I got to my desk, ready to handle whatever was waiting for me. By afternoon, my boss had not come into the office nor had he checked in, and I didn't know what to think. I had no idea where he was. I called his cell but got no answer. I finally called the New York office and found out that he was expected to be there all week. Yet, he'd never said a word to me. No phone call, no email, nothing. How easy would it have been to leave me a message or send me an email? Was I no longer an important member of his team?

I thought about how it had been in the past. I used to run his entire office and his schedule at Disney. I had just left Disney because I did not feel valued by my new boss there; it was my main reason for leaving. He had definitely underutilized me and my skill set. But that had never been the case in the past, so what was going on? This was certainly odd and completely out of character for how our relationship had worked up to this point. And another peculiar thing, as totally involved and controlling of his entire schedule as I had been at Disney, I'd been told when I started at the law firm that there would be no need to open or monitor his emails or phone calls. Now that was particularly strange.

The next week when he returned to the office, he called me in and told me to shut the door. "I probably should have told you this before you came back to work with me, but we're moving over to another law firm in December." *Seriously! I mean seriously! Um, yeah, you think he could have mentioned that before I uprooted from Disney?* As unhappy as I'd become working there, it had been difficult to consider leaving Disney. Now, after making the decision to return to the law firm we'd previously worked at together, I was being told we were moving again—this time to something completely unknown.

We left just before the holidays. The kicker was that they withheld my final paycheck since I had taken vacation time that technically I had not accrued. I started thinking I was getting screwed. What I didn't know was that this was just the beginning.

The first whack upside the head in transitioning to another law firm was not only the continued traffic nightmare, but parking was in a lot across the street from the building. I now had to pay for my own parking—quite the comedown from having my own parking spot in the executive parking structure on the studio lot at Disney. After a week or so of settling in, my boss was off to New York again. I had to tackle the tedious task of reformatting his client list, which we brought from Disney and the previous law firm. Everything had been uploaded to his cell phone. The law firm's IT person downloaded it to my computer, and I spent hours cleaning it up and updating all the phone numbers and contact information so we could upload the corrected information back to his cell phone.

When he returned to the office, he was able to connect his cell phone to update the information. After he did this, he complained to me that the information was still wrong, and it needed to be fixed. IT had no idea what the problem was. I went back in and started over again, trying to make sure everything was properly updated, but again, he instructed that I needed to "fix it now."

Once again, I spent hours updating and correcting all the contact information. I knew I had already done this, but at least this project kept me somewhat busy, albeit frustrated. When he uploaded the information again to his cell, the same thing happened. All the information reverted to the original incorrect data. I finally figured out what might be happening and asked IT if they had changed his phone to receive updated information and not be the primary source of information to download to the computer. It turned out that every time my boss connected his device as the primary source, the law firm computer would accept all the old information as primary and change back everything I had just cleaned. It took me, a non-IT person, to figure this out. Why didn't the "experts" know to look at which device had been designated as the primary device? I started to wonder if this law firm was the right place for me.

Not long after we arrived, one of the named partners in the firm asked me when my boss would be back in the LA office. He wanted to set up some meetings with prominent clients. I told him I would have to check. It was embarrassing for me not to know his schedule down to the minute, but in this case, I really had no idea when he would be back in LA. Life was very different than it used to be working together, and I was beginning to think that I had made a huge mistake by leaving Disney. Sometimes the devil you know is better than the devil you don't know.

One thing that occasionally kept me busy was doing his expense reports, especially because he was traveling so much. The first inconsistency I noticed was the inordinate amount of phone charges he was racking up while flying from LA to New York. One charge was for several hundred dollars! I knew he wasn't working on any cases, so who was he talking to? What I soon came to find out was that he was spending all the time on the cross-country flight talking with a partner from our previous law firm. He would call her from the plane and talk for hours.

While I had no concrete evidence that anything was going on other than interacting for professional reasons, I had a gut feeling that it was more than just legal discussions. That information was the impetus I needed to say my goodbyes. I now understood why he'd become so distant and kept all of his comings and goings private, but I could no longer work for someone who I could not stand behind and support. After only being back with him for four and a half months, I gave my notice in February. I was done. I felt used and betrayed.

It was time to leave corporate life. I had no idea what I would do next, but I knew I couldn't stay. Our relationship was truly not the same, nor would it ever be again. After I quit, I never heard from him. I reached out a few times over the years, but he never responded. I have, however, stayed in touch with his ex-wife (yes, they did divorce).

PART TWO

The Audacity of Tenacity

CHAPTER 10

A New Direction

*Embrace the opportunities presented and
learn from them.*

DURING MY LAST FEW MONTHS AT DISNEY, I started
taking classes to get my massage therapy certification. I looked at
this as possible "elective employment" for someday in the future. I
knew I'd always enjoyed getting a massage, so becoming a massage
therapist seemed to be a way I could bring joy to others as well. I
completed my course requirements, sat for the National Massage
Therapy Boards, and received my national license.

After resigning from the law firm, I decided to focus on creat-
ing a massage business. Segueing from a full-time corporate job

with a steady paycheck, benefits, and perks to a solo entrepreneur with no self-marketing experience is not for the faint of heart. It is really difficult—at least it was for me. As a nationally certified, licensed massage therapist, I started working at a local day spa. I loved working with the clients, but there were often big gaps in my schedule. For instance, I might have one client in the morning then nothing until four o'clock. It was frustrating, to say the least. After a few months at the spa, I was given basic instruction on how to provide lymph massage. Knowing that the training they provided was not enough and acknowledging that I certainly was not certified, I was uncomfortable performing a service I felt unqualified to offer, so I gave my notice.

I procured a few private clients, and that meant driving to the clients' houses and schlepping around a seventy-five-pound table from car to client and back again. I charged by the hour, but that did not include travel time. What was I thinking?

Looking for an easier and more lucrative arrangement, I attempted to go back to Disney and the law firm where I'd last been working to gain chair massage clientele. Goodness knows, Disney executives, their assistants, and the attorneys and their assistants certainly needed it. It seemed like a great idea to locate myself for a number of hours where I could serve a solid base of clients. I thought that by offering a much-needed service, I would be booked out each time I was on-site. It turned out to be just the opposite. It was a constant chore to regularly book a conference room and clients at each place. I ended up with one or two regulars at Disney and none at the law firm. It was a lot of work for twenty dollars for twenty minutes. I knew I had to rethink this path, and that's when a chance meeting led me to further guidance: horses.

It was January 2007, and I was out walking my two dogs, Sierra and Takota, around my neighborhood. A woman in a pickup truck stopped, introduced herself, said she lived in the neighborhood, and asked if I wanted company walking my dogs. This was not an everyday occurrence, and actually quite unusual. I did not even know the names of my next-door neighbors, so to have someone stop and engage in conversation was a bit strange. But I said, "Sure, why not?" and from then on, Eve and I met two times a week to walk my dogs.

After a week or two, she asked me if I liked horses. Of course I did. I had always wanted my own horse. As a young girl, I watched *My Friend Flicka* and *Bonanza* (for the horses, not the Cartwright boys) on television. Queens Village, New York, where I grew up, was not a prime area to own a horse. And riding lessons were out of the question. Eve said she had two horses boarded at the stable just up the road from our gated community. She could not ride, and she had to walk each of the horses on the trails around the facility. It would be a great help to her if I could join her and walk one of the horses.

I jumped at the opportunity. The first time I drove onto Marshall Canyon Boarding Facility, I was so excited I could barely contain myself. Eve met me and took me to meet Smarty—a beautiful chestnut registered American Quarter Horse. She was stunning, and I was immediately in love. As we walked the trails, I started getting to know Smarty while Eve walked Ruby, her favorite gelding. After a few weeks of walking Smarty, Eve let me ride her. I truly was in heaven.

Eve taught me to saddle up and lunge her before I got on. By July of that year, I owned Smarty, my first-ever horse! And on November 13, 2007—my fiftieth birthday—I went for my first-ever, all-by-myself trail ride. It was glorious riding out of the property on a beautiful California day, all alone on the mountain trail, on the back of a horse. That was truly the most connected to Spirit I had ever experienced.

I was up at the stables almost every day, either grooming Smarty or lunging her to get some exercise. At most boarding facilities, if the owner does not come up to get the horse out of its stall, it stands in a ten-foot by twelve-foot box day and night. I made it a priority to get up there as often as I could to make sure she got out—and to bond with my new love.

Energy healing is a traditional healing system that restores the balance and flow of energy throughout the body, mind, and soul. This technique works directly with the physical, emotional, and spiritual aspects of well-being and can be used on humans as well as animals. One day, not long after I acquired Smarty, as I massaged her and did some energy work on her, I felt as though we were being watched. I looked up from her stall and saw that almost every other horse in the barn aisle was watching what I was doing, and I heard, "Ooh, can I be next?" That got me thinking, and after taking a long, deep breath, I came to the conclusion that it was time to head back to school to get certified in equine body-work, something I knew existed but hadn't considered doing, that is, not until that day.

The longer I was away from the day-to-day corporate grind, the more aware I was becoming of my innate ability to listen to my intuition. Spending more and more time out of the house, in nature, and around horses was opening me up to connection with Spirit and my personal soul purpose. I had a strong feeling that equine bodywork certification was the next step on my continuing journey to find my true purpose.

During my horse bodywork training, there were plenty of horses to practice on. One of the first horses I worked with was Big Jake. Jake was a huge Percheron, a draft horse with hooves the size of dinner plates. Because his stall was much too small a space to safely work in, I took Jake out to the round pen. I also made sure I brought in the mounting block for something to stand on. Otherwise I would never be able to reach and work along Jake's spine.

I started massaging Jake, and he was definitely curious about what was going on. After I finished one side along his spine, he walked away and left me standing on the block in the middle of the round pen. He stood over by the fence. Someone walked by and asked what I was doing, wondering if I needed help. Listening to my inner voice, I intuitively knew and trusted that Jake was doing what he needed to do to get the full benefit of the massage and energy work I had just shared with him. I knew I did not need help and responded, "No thanks. I'm waiting for Jake to process." With that, Jake gave a full-body shake and came back to me, positioning himself so I could now work on his other side. Jake showed me just how smart horses are.

Equine Bodywork (EBW) certification was a multiyear process. I had to learn all of the muscles in a horse, as well as the bone structure. As a final "test" for my certification, I was required to videotape a complete body massage and send it in for evaluation. Luckily, at Marshall Canyon Boarding Facility, I had plenty of "clients" to practice on. I aced my test on the first submission and became a certified equine bodyworker.

Because horses give so much to humans, I thought it would be wonderful for me to be able to give some healing to them in return. Unfortunately, after I was certified and looking for actual paying clients, things dried up. This was 2008 during the financial recession. I knew money was tight for many people and paying for a massage and bodywork for a horse was definitely not a top priority.

No matter the circumstances of those times, though, I was definitely connecting more deeply to my relationship with horses. The best way I can illustrate my deep and profound connection is actually something my husband said. My dad had come to visit us, and while he was there, Peter and I drove Dad to church each Sunday. We waited in the parking lot and then took him to breakfast afterward.

One Saturday, I was invited to join two other horse owners on a trail ride the following day. I said I'd have to let them know because I needed to take Dad to church. When I told Peter, he said, "No, you go ahead. I'll take Dad to church and breakfast. No problem." I was thrilled and met up with Deanne and Tracy for our ride the next morning.

As Peter drove Dad to church, he mentioned to Peter something about me no longer going to church, and Peter responded, "Ray, every time she is out on the trails on the back of a horse, she is in church." *That was it exactly!* I had come to know that there was something spiritual between me, my horse, and nature while I was riding out on the trails, but I had never connected it with anything tangible. Thankfully, my husband did.

One of my wonderful canine companions, Sierra, passed away, and not long after, I went to work on a favorite client, a handsome paint gelding named Quinn. As I greeted him and walked over to begin my work, he walked away. I thought that was different, so I gave him a moment and then walked over to try again. Once more he walked away. I turned my back to him and examined my own energy to determine if he was feeding off something I was emanating. While my back was turned, he walked over, put the center of his forehead (his third eye chakra) against the middle of my shoulder blades (my heart chakra), and I heard very distinctly, "You need healing more than I do today. I can wait until you are ready."

Quinn knew I was not over the loss of my Sierra, and he helped me heal. As I stood in his stall, he circled around me and again put his forehead in the center of my back. In "energy speak," Quinn was sending healing energy directly into my hurting heart.

After completing my EBW certification, I wanted to find a consistent way to give back to horses, so I began volunteering at a therapeutic riding stable. Every other week, I drove the hour out to the stable and met the barn manager, Cathy. She would give me an update on the horses and tell me who needed some work. It was a wonderful thing to see the special partnership between horse and therapy rider. Therapeutic riding horses will literally hold themselves out of alignment to keep their riders safe. My part of this partnership was to bring massage, bodywork, and energy healing to these horses so they could continue to provide their own healing work for years to come.

On one particular day as I was finishing up my body and energy work, Cathy came over and said, "Before you leave, can you talk to our new mare, Buttercup? She just got here about a week ago and is not easy to work with."

Loving the opportunity to tap into my animal communication gifts that were becoming more and more apparent to me, I put my bag down and went over to the new mare. She was standing way back from the gate with her butt to the door. I grounded and centered myself by stopping where I was, closing my eyes, taking a deep slow breath, and asking my spirit guides to be with me. Then I approached Buttercup, introduced myself, and asked her how we could help her get more comfortable with being at the stable. She looked over her shoulder at me, and I distinctly heard, "My name." I asked, "What about your name?" She responded, "Buttercup. I am not a Buttercup. Buttercup is the name of a child's pony."

I got the feeling that she knew she was much more than that. I waited a few moments, checked with my intuition, and said, "You are so right. I believe you are quite the lady. In fact, that is a wonderful name. How about Lady or Lady Grace?" She turned around, came right over to the gate, and put her head on my chest. "Ooh, I like that. Will you tell the others?" I told Cathy about the requested name change, and as soon as I got home, I sent an email to the owner with the request. Being an open-minded person, she readily accepted the name change and told all the volunteers that going forward, her mare was to be called Lady Grace.

Two weeks later, Cathy met me at the entrance to the stable and told me that Lady Grace was a changed horse. She enjoyed her work, paid attention to requests, and was acting like quite the lady. As I walked past her stall, Lady Grace stuck out her head and said, "Thank you."

CHAPTER 11

Begin Again–Despite the Prognosis

Pay attention to messages from Spirit, or you might get whacked upside the head.

I WAS AT MARSHALL CANYON tending to Smarty when Debi, another boarder, approached me. She mentioned that her family would be moving and they were going to take her daughter's show horse but would not be taking their other horse, Bodie, with them.

She said to me, "I've seen the change in Smarty since you've started working with her, and I was hoping you would be able to adopt Bodie and work with him too." Debi told me that she was feeling guilty about leaving Bodie behind. Yet, after watching the change in Smarty's caring and confidence since I had acquired her, she believed Bodie would be in excellent hands if I agreed to take him. She knew I would not just leave him in his stall all week and only take him out on weekends, like some people treated their horses that were boarded there.

That was quite the compliment. Since Smarty was my first-ever horse, I literally was learning as I went. The fact that she saw improvement in Smarty told me I was doing something right. Besides availing myself of the wisdom of others, training and research, I also seemed to have an innate knowledge of what training and education was best for both me and the horse. I was excited for the opportunity to partner with Bodie and see how different he was from Smarty and how I would need to adjust my care and training to accommodate his needs.

I talked it over with Peter, and we acquired our second horse, *Bodhi* (yes, the first thing I did was change the spelling of his name), with the intent for him to become Peter's trail-riding horse. I felt compelled to change the spelling of Bodie's name to give him a fresh start at a new life. My inner voice told me he was a special horse, and I know there are no coincidences. Bodie came into my life for a reason, and I felt that by changing the spelling to Bodhi, I enabled him to embrace his inner *bodhisattva*. A *bodhisattva* embodies the compassion of all Buddhas as one who is able to reach nirvana but compassionately delays doing so in order to save suffering beings. My Bodhi would play an integral role in my own journey to healing and enlightenment.

Bodhi had had a difficult life. Prior to us, he had experienced a severe accident where he got his head caught between the stall door and the wall. Tomas, our regular barn manager, was on vacation at the time, and the person filling in for him had closed Bodhi's stall door but did not chain it tight. It created some space when the door was pushed. Anyone who knows horses knows that they will push open doors whenever they can, in order to find more hay.

Apparently, Bodhi stuck his head through the opening and then did not realize that he needed to lift his head up and over the door to dislodge himself. Sadly, he was stuck that way all night. Someone finally found him in the morning, hanging in the doorway. He had nerve damage to his neck and the side of his face. His lip hung down on one side. When he became part of our family, I performed massage and energy work on him every day. He'd been with us for about four months and his lip was almost completely healed by the time I had my own accident.

The first time I rode Bodhi was an illuminating experience. I saddled him up and took him to the round pen. Just as Eve had taught me, I ran him around a bit to loosen up the cinch. We walked over to the mounting block, and I tightened up the cinch again. I got on and off we went. Well, not quite. We walked around the boarding facility, and what I first noticed was that when I asked him to stop, he did, but then he started walking backward. This is not a good thing to have happen if you're on a trail with a drop-off of any kind on either side. I realized we needed to work on this. Off we went again. As we passed one of the barn stall aisles, he started moving sideways up the aisle. *Well, this is new*, I thought. *Something else we will need to address before we go out on a trail ride.*

During those initial months, I worked with Bodhi as often as I could. I wanted to be able to trust him to pay attention to what the rider was asking before I let Peter ride him. Our mutual education was going well until one fateful day in September.

Knowing who you are and, perhaps more importantly, where you are is tantamount to our very existence and well-being. Yet, awareness is something we usually take for granted. On this particular day, however, my awareness became extremely important to me when I began to realize that I was lying in a bed that was not my own.

Confusion set in further as three friends I used to work with at the California Chapter of the American Massage Therapy Association came into focus. *Why are they here in my bedroom?* I wondered. *And wait, this is actually* not *my bedroom. What the f___ is going on?*

"Hi. What are you guys doing here? And where are we?" I asked out loud. Scanning the room, I noticed I was in a single bed positioned behind a glass partition. There was a lot of activity beyond the partition, but the details of the activity did not register. I turned to the other side of the room and saw my brother, Chris. Chris lives in Massachusetts, clear across the country from me. Now I was even more confused. None of what I was seeing made any sense.

"What are *you* doing here? And *where are we*?" I asked more loudly. That's when I realized that I had a tube in my nose and wires in my arm as well as in other places. *What the heck is going on?* Finally seeing my wonderful husband, Peter, I knew I was safe, but that still did not explain things.

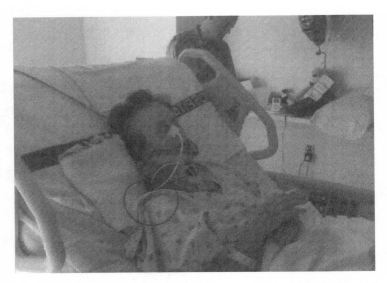

Peter told me (not for the first time, apparently) that I'd been in a riding accident, and I was in the ICU. I'd been there for three weeks. *Oh my gosh, that can't be right! Three weeks of my life gone. No, this must be a mistake. I'm fine. Get these tubes and wires off me. Let me go home. I want to see my dog. Peter, take me home.*

Unfortunately, that was not an option. While I did not comprehend the severity, I found out that during the past few weeks in the ICU, I had been in and out of consciousness (none of which I remember, which I would later learn is quite common). My incredible sister, Claudia, had been there with Peter and me for the first difficult week of medical decisions. Since she is a registered nurse, Claudia was able to help Peter understand the medical jargon, and she made sure I was well cared for. She also kept me as dry as possible because for a period of time, the doctors required me to be packed in ice to keep my temperature down. Claudia also made sure the nursing staff knew I was a vegetarian (not that I was eating anything at the time).

One side of my head had been shaved, and a dime-sized hole had been made to put a shunt in my skull. A probe had been inserted into my brain to monitor my intercranial pressure (ICP). If the ICP exceeded a certain number, they would have to operate to relieve the pressure buildup on my brain. I am grateful to Spirit that I did not require surgery. The technical medical term of my diagnosis was a traumatic brain injury.

After more days of recovering my awareness, I learned the following about what had occurred: It had been a beautiful Southern California fall day—not too hot—and the sun was shining, with the scent of dry brush and a subtle sage wafting on the breeze. Bodhi, my eighteen-year-old quarter horse gelding, and I were attempting to go on a trail ride.

I had been working with him to establish trust in me and to relax as we rode in the round pen and the arena on the boarding facility property. We had not yet gone out on the trails surrounding the facility, since Bodhi continued to display the troublesome habit of backing up whenever I asked him to stop. He would stop, then start to back up slowly, despite my encouragement to stay still. I'd been focusing on changing this behavior that could prove fateful for both of us on a riding trail. By September, I believed he was ready to move beyond the confined spaces where we'd been diligently working hard.

What I learned months later through my friend and animal communicator, Cindy Hartzell, was that Bodhi refused to go out on the trail that day and kept bringing us back to the office at the boarding facility. Lori, one of the facility employees, heard someone "fussing with a horse." She came out of the office to see what was going on and saw me on Bodhi in an emergency stop. Since we were not moving, she thought nothing of it, and was ready to turn and go back into the office, when she watched me come off Bodhi, making no attempt to break my fall. Bodhi was standing still as I came off.

What Lori realized later was that when she first saw me, I had no expression. Not angry, not scared, not pissed. Nothing. She noted that there seemed to be "no one home." Had I experienced a seizure? A stroke? Since I arrived at the emergency trauma center from a "horse accident," those possibilities were never explored.

Emergency paramedics were called to the facility, and after preliminary determination, they made the decision to transport me to a local hospital. That is, until I got combative. As the EMTs tried to conduct their initial evaluation, they had already placed a neck brace on me and were proceeding to remove my clothes to determine if anything was broken or traumatized before they strapped me to a body board. That is when I got combative and started fighting as best I could.

Apparently when a patient gets combative with EMTs, they must consider the possibility of brain trauma. They immediately changed their decision to transport me to a local hospital and called for air transport to take me to the nearest (and best, thank goodness) trauma center. When I learned of this many weeks later, I thought, *Well, of course I got combative. I had three guys trying to cut off my clothes ... you would get combative too.*

After they made the determination of a possible brain injury, I was airlifted by helicopter to LAC/USC Medical Center Trauma Unit. I was later told that I'd been put on a body board and transported to a nearby soccer field so that the helicopter could land safely and had room to maneuver. I am extremely thankful that I have no memory of this, as I have an extreme aversion to helicopters. I arrived at LAC/USC without identification or confirmation that I had medical insurance, so I was admitted but initially only received basic trauma care to stabilize me.

Luckily, the two women who cared for our horses whenever we were on vacation were at the stables just after my accident. When they heard what happened to me, and after learning that Peter was out of town, Marion and Kristen went to my tack shed, got my purse and wallet, found my medical insurance card, and drove to the hospital. Because these two angels had the wherewithal to bring my medical information to the hospital, I was immediately transferred to the ICU and major testing and care truly began.

By the time the helicopter took off, the owner and manager of Marshall Canyon Boarding Facility had called Peter, who was attending meetings in New Jersey at his company's headquarters. Trying not to panic, Peter immediately contacted his travel department and told them what was going on, all the while trying to figure out what he needed to do first. His travel department interrupted him and said they would handle everything. They made arrangements for him to fly directly into Los Angeles Airport and had a car ready to drive him to the hospital. He told them his car was at Ontario Airport, which was closer to our home, and they explained that the car and driver would wait for Peter and drive him to his car whenever he needed it. We were both blessed that Peter's employer, Johnson & Johnson, took control of the travel arrangements necessary to get Peter to my side as quickly as possible.

Peter arrived at my ICU room very late that first night. He walked in, took my hand, and said, "Honey, it's me. I'm here. You're going to be okay." Awhile after he spoke those words, Peter told me I finally turned my head toward him and said, "It's about damn time." That one sentence told my husband everything he needed to know: yes, his feisty, at times sarcastic, wife was still here.

The next day, Claudia arrived in order to support Peter and help navigate the medical decisions that would be required. It had already been determined that I had cracked my left occipital bone and sustained a right frontal hematoma. I was on anti-seizure medication, and the procedure was approved to shave one-half of my head and insert the intracranial pressure monitor.

Over the three weeks I was in the ICU, I was in and out of consciousness. At times I could answer easy yes-or-no questions, but by the following day, I would not even be able to squeeze Peter's hand when asked for a response. It was truly a roller-coaster ride for my husband and family. One bright spot was what I like to think of as my hold on humor. Apparently, I could not remember how to tell them that my feet were cold. But I could remember the words to a 1976 Michael Franks song "Popsicle Toes," which I would sing when I wanted socks.

After Claudia had to leave to get back to her own job and family, my brother, Chris, flew in to support Peter. By this time, it was determined that I might be there for a while, so I was intubated with a nasal gastric tube in order to receive nourishment. Chris gave the nutrition, which looked like a vanilla milkshake and had the amusing name of "spooge." Whenever the bag was empty, he would alert the nurses that "she needs more spooge." He made sure I was "eating," which was one less thing Peter had to deal with. I am so grateful to both of my siblings for flying out to "circle the wagons" when Peter and I were in need.

CHAPTER 12

Rehabilitation

*All it takes is faith, trust, and a
belief in your own strength.*

AFTER THREE WEEKS IN THE ICU, I spent four weeks at
Casa Colina Hospital and Centers for Healthcare in Pomona,
California. This facility was much closer to our house, and that
meant Peter was able to visit every afternoon and still be home at
night to take care of his basic needs and our dog, Takota.

Because I still could not comprehend the severity of my
injury, the day before my transfer out of the ICU, I was lying in
my ICU bed, exploring the wires and tubes attached to me. The
one in my nose was the most annoying, and while Peter was out

of the room, I made the brilliant decision to pull out my nasogastric tube. I didn't understand why it was there. I had been lying in bed for three weeks, having things done to and for me. I'd had no input, no sense of control, and no choice about what was going on. As far as this tube was concerned, I could make a decision—I took control and started pulling.

It came out easily, even though it felt weird coming up and out of my esophagus. This body part is not something that technically should be in your circle of awareness, and yet I could feel this tube snaking its way up my throat and out my nose. *Very peculiar.*

Peter was clearly not happy to see what I had accomplished. I thought it was brilliant and did not understand his annoyance. He spoke to my head nurse, who explained to him that I was being transferred to a new hospital, and they could definitely reintubate me if necessary. In fact, she told him, they probably would have removed it anyway to see if I was able to swallow. *Ha! Vindicated.* I had saved them a step.

The transfer to Casa Colina was relatively uneventful. Peter came with me in the ambulance, and Chris drove Peter's car behind us. I could see Chris in the car out the back window of the ambulance and got confused seeing my brother driving my husband's car behind the vehicle we were traveling in. Because my brain was in the early stages of healing, multitasking was impossible, and most processing of any kind took time, focus, and a lot of energy. Since this event made no sense, I decided not to try and figure it out, and instead, closed my eyes and rested.

Once in my room at Casa Colina, I was in another new environment with a new routine. Peter stayed as long as he could while I was settled in and they performed their initial assessment of my needs. The first determination was that I would not need to be reintubated with a nasogastric tube, and I would be evaluated the next day as to what I could ingest, if anything. They also determined that I would not have a catheter reinserted either.

That first night in my new environment was time for me to do my own evaluation. What did this injury mean to me and the rest of my life? How would I recover? Even more important, how much would I recover? First things first, I had to pee, so I decided to take myself to the bathroom. As I maneuvered out of bed, I heard an alarm go off. *What the heck? That is annoying. Where is it coming from?* Exploring the buttons and lights on the equipment at the bottom of the bed, I quickly figured out how to turn off the alarm and then headed for the bathroom. I was feeling rather good about my ability to manage things for myself.

As I came out of the bathroom, however, the night nurse was there, glaring at me. "Terri, what are you doing?" she asked. *Duh, pretty obvious*, I thought. "I went to the bathroom," I responded. She slowly explained to me that I was to ring for help if I needed to use the facilities and wait until someone came to help me.

I'd been going to the bathroom by myself since I was potty-trained decades ago, so why would I need company now? I did not realize that I'd been labeled a "fall risk" and needed to wait for assistance for all activities that required me to get out of bed.

After a slight discussion, she agreed that I could go to the bathroom by myself. *Yay, another victory!* But this would not be the last time I was admonished by the nursing staff for testing my boundaries.

On that first night alone in this new facility, I "felt" the presence of my dog, Sierra. Sierra had passed one year earlier, but I knew her spirit was with me on the bed by my feet. When I closed my eyes, I could even see her with me. It was a much-needed comfort to know she was with me and that I was truly not alone.

It was strange to now be aware of where I was and what was happening. It made for long hours while I waited for physical or speech therapy. My new routine included speech therapy every afternoon, and physical and/or cognitive therapy once a day. For the rest of the time, I stayed in my room with nothing to do. I had access to a TV, but no books or computer, leaving me with plenty of time to think, wonder, ponder, and explore why this had happened and what I would do with this "new" brain function. Would I be "damaged" for the rest of my life? Would I be able to drive again? Most importantly, would I be able to ride my horses? Sleeping was a welcome time killer and very much needed for my brain to repair itself.

My first meeting with Chad, my speech therapist, went well, until he had to evaluate me for swallowing. I had to drink a thick "liquid" to make sure I could swallow correctly and get the liquid into my esophagus and not my lungs. Yuck! But if I were to "graduate" to real food, I needed to prove to Chad that I could at least swallow liquid correctly and safely.

One caveat was that I could not use a straw. He was concerned that my "sucking reflex" had been compromised. Not only did he need to determine whether I could swallow, but he needed to see that my epiglottis was working correctly and that I was not going to take food or liquid into my larynx and lungs. So initially, there would be no straws. Annoying, but not the end of the world. And this was when I came up with a favorite statement: "Well, if that is the worst thing that happens today, then not so bad." I still use that statement today.

Almost a week later, Chad gave me the approval to use a straw. I was so happy, I called Peter and shared the good news. When Peter came to visit me that afternoon, he brought me my favorite beverage: a Starbucks Vanilla Bean Frappuccino—complete with a straw. Oh, happy day! My life in the hospital was finally looking up. There was a light at the end of the tunnel.

Physical and cognitive therapies were learning opportunities for me. Initially, I was not allowed to do or go anywhere on my own, so I was transferred to a wheelchair and taken to my appointments. I acquiesced and adhered to the rules.

Since I had not broken anything other than my head, physical therapy was easy—walking and stairs to get my muscles back into acceptable parameters. Cognitive therapy was strange, though. For one of the activities, I had to move little cars and trucks around a board without hitting anything else on the board. I'm guessing it was to have me practice eye-hand coordination and see if I knew the difference between a car and a truck and also the color of the vehicle. I do remember not being very good at it when I initially started.

After just a few days, I was encouraged to practice getting into the wheelchair on my own, and if I felt up to it, to use my arms to move the wheels and scooch my feet to wheel myself around the hallways. I did this a time or two and realized what I wanted to do instead was put on my sneakers and push the wheelchair in front of me as I walked behind to do laps around the hallway.

Even though I was not yet "authorized" to walk on my own, I needed to move, and this was a great and safe way to do it on my own. Or so I thought. I also knew I was not going to be completely alone, as Sierra's spirit always walked with me. I had been lying in bed for three weeks, and I was overwhelmed with the need to move. Although this was not the "prescribed" method for me to move, I kept taking my walks and pushing my wheelchair, with Sierra by my side. Somehow, deep inside I knew what would best help me, and I listened to that inner guidance.

The highlight of my second week in the rehab hospital was when Peter arrived one afternoon and told me to put on my sneakers because we were going for a ride. He helped me get into my wheelchair and then proceeded to push me out into the hospital courtyard. Finally, I was outside in the sunshine and natural warmth of the day. I was in heaven. He "parked" me in the sun and said he had a surprise, but I had to promise not to get out of my chair. Of course, I said, "No problem. I promise to stay here and enjoy the sun." Off he went while I waited, enjoying that I was outside of the hospital with all its medicinal smells and constant activity.

After a few minutes, I saw Peter walking toward me, and much to my surprise and delight, he had Takota with him. My fur baby was coming toward me, trying to move much faster than the leash would allow. This would be the first time in almost two months for me to receive dog kisses and cuddles.

As they got closer, I stood up and slid out of my chair to sit on the ground, breaking my promise to stay in the chair so I could better embrace Takota's wriggling body. Peter saw how happy I was, and when he was close enough, he let go of Takota's leash and she came running to me. It was absolutely wonderful. I cried tears of joy and love. Although I'd had Sierra's spirit energy around me, this was different. This was forty pounds of unconditional love in my lap.

After four weeks at the rehab hospital, I had improved enough to be transferred to Casa Colina Transitional Living Center. This facility was a standalone building, yet connected to the hospital.

Each day was filled with intensive therapy sessions, which focused on:

- Physical restoration of functions, including bowel and bladder control, mobility, and self-care;

- Cognitive skill-building, addressing attention, concentration, memory, problem-solving, and communication;

- Social/behavioral shaping, improving impulse control, social appropriateness, and frustration tolerance;

- Reintegration into the home and community, covering home skills, money management, accessing transportation, and safety awareness; and

- Psychological adjustment, addressing changes in relationships, body image, and living with a new sense of self.

I was happy to learn that I would be placed in a higher functioning group; however, one downside of being in the transitional living center was that almost all of the therapies and activities were conducted in a group setting. We were assigned to a group of four or five patients, and this group had a daily schedule of activities and therapies. Since I was labeled "high functioning," I rarely had one-on-one therapy of any kind. All meals were at the same time in the communal dining room. And any TV watching was decided by whoever got the TV remote first. It always seemed to be a group of male patients watching some sporting event. The entire group process was quite challenging for a high introvert like me. I spent a lot of time reading. And frequently, I had to read the same page over and over before I understood what I was reading.

One of the first things scheduled was a meeting with the clinical neuropsychologist and director of the facility. He explained to me that before my injury, my brain function was probably at a level eight. After the brain injury, my function was at maybe a level two. He stated that after about two more years of rehab, I might get to a level four or five.

I left that meeting confused and with a lump in my throat. All I wanted to do was get back to my bed so I could digest what I'd just been told about my prognosis. *Is this really true? Is this going to be my future? Functioning but barely? Unable to have more than one thought at a time? Not able to drive myself? What a burden I will be on Peter. This cannot be true.* I sat up in my bed, looked around the room, and said out loud, "Bullshit, this is not the end of me. I'm only fifty-two. I'm not done yet. I stayed on the planet for a reason, dammit, and I'm not going to give up on my life. It's time to really start over and begin again."

I realized that I was only blocked by the power of my own thoughts. And my thought right then and there was: *I can still do anything I put my mind to. I will take the time I need to heal and get stronger.* I knew the brain is an amazing organ and that we still don't know all it can achieve. I was not going to let some guy (no matter how many letters he had after his name) dictate to me how broken I was or how broken I would remain. I chose to believe I would completely heal. After all, I stayed on the planet for an important mission, not to sit around feeling sorry for my life and not living my soul's purpose.

After processing my "prognosis," the first thing I did was set up a daily morning routine. At the transitional living center, everyone had to share a room. I do not share well, especially when the setting is noisy. My roommate, Susan, was a smoker recovering from a stroke. She coughed and hacked all through the night. It was not the best environment for my own recovery. When I mentioned my lack of sleep at one of my doctor follow-ups, I was told, "Oh, you're not sleeping? We can prescribe a pill for that." I tried to explain I couldn't sleep because of the noise and interruptions during the night. If I could be moved to a single room, that would solve my problem. I did not want to start on sleeping medications. No unnecessary meds for me, thank you. I politely declined the offer for medication and was told that no one had a single room, so I could not be moved.

Each morning, I awoke early, took a shower and dressed, then left the room and made my way to the kitchen where Maria, one of the early morning shift attendants, was normally busy cleaning up the room and getting ready for the breakfast meal delivery. I usually made small talk with Maria, made myself a cup of tea, got two packages of graham crackers, and curled up in the window nook to read. At this point, I still frequently had to read a paragraph two or three times before I could move on, but at least I wasn't lying around in bed all morning feeling pitiful.

I also asked Peter to bring me my computer. He was skeptical and made me promise I would not be doing any kind of work on it. An easy promise to make! I wanted it so that I could play matching games to work on my eye-hand coordination and stamina. My favorite was Chuzzle, a tile-matching video game, because you had to match these adorable puffy things with googly eyes by color. I played every afternoon. Because my brain was still healing, I could not focus for more than a half hour or so. Since my Chuzzle skills were at a low level, I never did make it past losing my five Chuzzle lives quickly.

While at the center, all patients were required to participate in physical therapy. Because I did not have any physical injuries to recover from, the therapists didn't know what to do with me. Most of the time, I was put on a treadmill and told to walk for twenty minutes and come find the physical therapist for something else to do afterward. It occurred to me that I was already functioning at a higher level than most others in the facility, and I was also coming from a better attitude. My mindset and belief were that even if I was "damaged," I could achieve anything with perseverance, determination, and patience. Many of the other patients had been in car accidents or survived strokes and were dealing with the challenges of recovering from broken bones or learning how to reuse speech or motor functions. Not everyone was a TBI-only survivor, like me.

As a patient who had been "promoted" into a higher functioning group, I was encouraged to attend outings. The first outing I was invited to attend was to McDonald's. I was a vegetarian, and it had been years since I'd been at a McDonald's. I politely declined the offer. Later that day, Peter pointed out that the outings were for a reason. They helped reacclimate a person into daily outside activities, and he thought I should participate. "Fine, I'll go on the next one," I told him.

Much to my horror, the next one was to IKEA. I truly dislike that store. If you've ever been in one, you know you can't get to where you want to go without having to walk through the entire store. I find the experience extremely annoying. But I went.

We were each given a list of five items that we had to find in the store and then write down the price for each item. Ack! But I had promised Peter I would be all-in. Off I went up the escalator and into the store. Walking through, I found an area set up like a living room, and there on the back of the sofa was one of my items. I sat down and wrote down the price. When I turned around, there on the coffee table was an IKEA catalog. *Eureka!* I started thumbing through the catalog when I heard my name. "Terri, what are you doing?" asked Rachel, our outing coordinator.

"I'm looking for my items," I replied.

"No, you're missing the point. You're supposed to navigate the store and find your items," she said.

"Rachel, not once in your instructions did you say we could not use the catalog."

She thought about that for a moment, smiled, and told me I was right, but then asked me to please physically go in search of the items throughout the store. I'm sure she made a note to change her instructions before the next group went to IKEA. What this outing showed me, beyond what they had planned, was that my brain was not broken, and I could still think outside the box. Feeling hopeful, I told myself that I just needed to continue healing and give my brain the time it needed to reweave the neural pathways back to optimum functioning.

CHAPTER 13

Home at Last

*Hold on with both hands to your positive
outlook—no matter what.*

EARLY ON IN MY REHABILITATION, a good friend shared
with me that during the time I was in the ICU, everyone had
been sending healing energy and praying for my full recovery.
She told me that while she was meditating one afternoon, she
met me in the "dream realm" and asked me if I wanted to come
back. I responded, "I don't know." Cindy said it was okay, and if
I chose not to come back, she and others would take care of Peter
and find good, loving homes for my horses. It was as if I was being
given permission to do whatever I needed to do. A week later, she

met me in the dream realm again, and I said, "I'm ready to come home." I woke up the following day and did not drift back into unconsciousness again.

After two months in the hospital and rehab, I was finally released and sent home. One of my first realizations after getting out of rehab was that my emotions were a bit off-kilter. Peter said it was as if my volume was either too high or too low. For instance, I reacted strongly to a joke. I had trouble processing and understanding some conversations, and many times I took things literally. To compensate, Peter took to announcing "humor alert" before making a comment.

Another side effect of my healing process was a serious lack of stamina. I had to take a nap every afternoon, and I told Peter "do not be concerned if I sleep a lot. I'm trying to catch up on all the interrupted sleep I experienced at the transitional living center."

Not only had I shared a room with a woman who coughed and hacked most of the night, but because she was recovering from a stroke, she also needed help to use the bathroom. When she asked for help during the night, someone would come into our room, turn on all the lights, and assist her, without any consideration for me as I tried to sleep. So I was definitely sleep-deprived, and I gave myself the opportunity to catch up by napping every afternoon.

In addition to my emotions being a bit "off," my brain processing was also off. One incident that illustrated how my brain processing had changed was right after I got home. Peter offered to make dinner, and the easiest for him was pasta. I walked into the kitchen, where he had my pasta pot on the gas stove with the burner turned up really high. What I saw were flames licking up the side of the pot. Whether that was true or not was not the point. I panicked and started flailing my hands while saying, "Oh ... oh ... flames, flames, flames." Peter turned down the heat, and I walked out of the kitchen, sat down on the sofa, and talked myself down from the ledge. *So, what will happen? The pot will burn. Then what? I'll have to buy a new pot. And then? No big deal, I get a new pasta pot.*

Peter watched my meltdown transpire but did not intervene. He let me process the event myself, and at dinner that night, I looked at him and said, "Wow, that was different." I was sincerely trying not to portray just how scared I was that my over-reaction to a relative non-event was going to be my new normal. Since I had talked myself off the ledge, Peter, too, was trying not to make a big deal of it. We discussed it, and I shared that I had no way to control my reactions and would need to let things happen. He shared that he did not know whether to jump in and take over or let me freak out, process, and reason myself to calmness. We decided it would be best for me to process whatever my reaction was, and he would do his best to support me, rather than react to my behavior as I figured things out. Unless, of course, safety was involved. Then he would definitely take over.

Soon, I was able to view and experience events with no judgment and no negativity. I accepted the fact that early in my healing process, I would be different.

It was another few weeks before I was able to see my horses. It took me that long before I felt strong enough, physically and emotionally, to go up to the barn. It had been more than two months since they had seen me. I'm sure they knew what was going on because they heard things. Animals also constantly communicate with each other and they absolutely understand what we humans are saying.

The day after Thanksgiving, Peter drove me up to the barn. He helped me out of the car, and we went to see Smarty. As alpha mare, she expected me to see her first. She was preoccupied with eating, but in between grabs of hay, she came over to the stall door where I was standing. She seemed rather unconcerned but happy to see me. Smarty placed her forehead down for me to scratch. She sniffed me from shaved head to my heart chakra. Making a "chuffeling" sound, she looked me in the eye, and I heard in my mind, "Nice to have you back. It's about time." Then she went back to eating.

Next it was time to see Bodhi. Since he was the horse I came off of, he knew a lot about what had happened. As we walked up to his stall, I noticed he was standing in the back with his head in the corner. I stood at the door and took a breath, then opened it and stepped in. He turned his head and looked, sadly, over his shoulder at me. When he saw it was me, he nickered, turned, and walked toward me slowly, with his head hanging down. I kept hearing, "I'm sorry. I didn't mean to hurt you. I'm sorry." He stood in front of me with his head still hanging. If horses could cry, I'm sure I would have seen tears rolling down his cheeks. I stepped up to him, put my arms around his neck, and said, "Dude, it's okay. I'm okay, and it was not your fault." He looked me in the eye, and I tried to convey that I was being honest with him. I did not, and still do not, blame him. He let out a big horsey sigh and leaned into me.

After just a few minutes of this connection, I felt him start to relax. He raised his head so his nostril was at my face. We breathed together. This sharing of breath is something horses do with each other when they are deeply connecting. They don't do it with humans very often. I knew this was Bodhi's way of reconnecting with me after all we both had been through. I felt completely accepted, broken brain and all.

With both horses, I felt their unconditional love and partnership. The smell of my horses, the sounds of chewing, and the feel of their weight and strength surrounded me with courage and protection. It was because of this special relationship that I forced myself up to the barn every morning to care for them and, most importantly, to learn about how my new brain wiring would work. I wanted to explore my deeper understanding of their communications and to receive their healing energy.

After the first week of this routine, I noticed that I was getting stronger and could *almost* do more than one thing at a time. For instance, I observed that I could continue to pick out hooves and say hello to someone walking by at the same time. When I first started my barn routine, I had to put the hoof down to concentrate on what someone was saying.

As the other boarders began to see me back at the facility, many wanted to stop and talk about the accident, how I was doing, and what I was going to do with Bodhi. Many felt it was his fault I had come off on my head. I told them what I knew, how I was progressing, and emphasized that it was *not* Bodhi's fault.

Not only were the horses helping me heal physically, but they were helping me heal emotionally and energetically. Because my balance was still slightly off (I tended to list to the left) and I did not want to scare Peter into thinking I was going to saddle up and go off on the trail by myself, I chose not to ride, but I was able to groom them and lunge them in the round pen. Just these small acts of caring for and exercising them gave me the feeling of "Yes, even though I may be somewhat dented, I am still whole and capable of being a productive human being."

I remember the first time I brushed Smarty after the accident. She has a fabulously long mane and tail, and to me, they smell like love. I buried my face in her mane, threw my arms around her neck, and thanked her for her strength, support, and patience.

Smarty took every opportunity to test my multitasking abilities, or in some cases, my lack thereof. She would move her head as I tried to put on her halter, causing me to have to move with her while trying to buckle the halter. Or she would purposefully bump into me while we walked, throwing me off balance. Some would chalk this up to the horse taking advantage of me, but I knew she was requiring me to up my game and force my brain to hurry up and heal the damaged neural pathways I needed to keep myself safe around the horses. She was an amazing "therapist."

The first time I saddled Smarty after the accident, I swear she had grown three inches, and my saddle had definitely gained weight. Not to mention the fact that as soon as I got the saddle on her, she started moving around. Saddling and cinching a moving target certainly afforded me the opportunity to increase my eye-hand coordination, whether I liked it or not. Apparently, she still had lessons to teach and healing to offer me. Together, we took every step on our journey, mine toward improved health, strength, patience, and understanding, and hers toward trusting that I would be with her every day.

After a month of doing only groundwork with Smarty and Bodhi, I felt ready to "get back on the horse" (literally) and take my first post-TBI ride. I was not ready to get on Bodhi, and neither was he, so my first time was with Smarty, wearing a riding helmet in the round pen. Peter was with me, too. I was nervous and so was Peter. I stepped up on the mounting block and had to stop to take a deep breath and try not to cry. I had always been confident on Smarty's back. Now I was scared. *What will happen? Will I panic? Will I fall off again?* I told myself that we were just going to be led around in the round pen, so there should be nothing to be afraid of. I took another deep breath and I did it. I took hold of the saddle horn, put one foot in the stirrup, and swung my leg over her back. Then I cried as Peter led us around like a big pony ride. For me, being out riding on the trail, just me and my horse, is when I am closest to Spirit, and my soul sings. The only way to experience that magnitude of connection to Spirit and my horse was to get back on. While the tears rolled down my cheeks as Peter led us slowly, I was grinning from ear to ear. Back in heaven!

As the days passed with my horses, I continued to be blessed with their healing energy. By caring for them, I increased my stamina, my strength, and my humor. Multitasking, although improving, could still cause a major glitch in my processing. When that happened, I'd smile at myself, take a deep breath, and figure out how to keep both myself and my horse safe.

As I continued to work with my horses, I had to reestablish my trust and relationship with each of them in different ways.

It took almost a full year before Bodhi and I learned to trust each other again. Eventually, he stopped feeling that he was a bad or dangerous horse. Today, he and I know, acknowledge, and honor the realization that he has played an integral part in my life's journey. If not for coming off him and landing on my head, I would not have had the opportunity to rewire the neural pathways in my brain. I would not have spent three weeks in and out of consciousness as I explored my spirituality and opened up to the realization that we (the horses and I) could help other life-challenged women and couples navigate their way back to their own life's journey and avoid living lives of quiet mediocrity.

Instead of looking at my accident as "Poor me, why did this happen?" I made the conscious choice to look at it as a necessary experience and an opportunity to rewire my brain, as well as to accept that I vibrate at a higher frequency than many others. How wonderful it has been to discover that I can understand horses, dogs, and other animals, on a deeper level, and I can share the horses' spirit, wisdom, and healing with people who are not able to connect with other beings in these ways.

CHAPTER 14

Returning to My Training

Give miracles the time they need to blossom.

NOT LONG INTO BEING a brand-new horse owner, I had attended a local equine affaire, which was a five-day equestrian exposition. I noticed on the schedule a demonstration by Melisa Pearce, who would be explaining the chakras of the horse. Now, that spoke to both my massage-energy-work language and my horse language. After watching the demo, I found Melisa in the vendor area, and we got to talking about all things energy, chakras, and horses. She invited me to participate in a phone call she had planned to introduce a new certification program called "Touched by a Horse," based on the Equine Gestalt Coaching Methodology (EGCM) she had created. This program would teach participants how to become a life coach who partnered with horses to the benefit of the human client.

I participated in the call and found out that it was a two-year program. Over the course of the next two years, in addition to weekly phone meetings, I would have to fly to Colorado eight times to Melisa's ranch for weekend intensives to learn how to coach other students while partnering with her horses.

I talked it over with Peter, and he asked, "What is it?"

"I have no idea," I responded, "but I know I have to do this."

It definitely was one of those serious intuitive hits that I knew was right.

I believe that certain circumstances, people, and animals come into our lives when we need them the most. Horses did not enter my life right after I left the corporate world. I had to gather the appropriate knowledge and life lessons before I was ready and open to the healing gifts of Equus. Led by intuition, I first became a certified massage therapist. Then I added energy balancing, reiki, and craniosacral therapy to my expanding massage and well-being toolbox. Next, I became an equine bodyworker to support the health of horses. Ultimately, I was presented with the opportunity to partner with horses and become an equine coach. I'd left the corporate world and found my way to my own path where I could support and care for horses, and they could do the same for me, so that together we could support and care for others. What a magical journey this turned out to be as I moved beyond a castle to an incredible life beyond my wildest dreams.

During my TBI recovery process, as I got stronger and more clear-headed, I began to realize that I was getting closer to the time when I could resume my equine coach training. I no longer had to take an afternoon nap every day. By that February, I was able to resume my "Touched by a Horse" equine coaching classes. I was halfway through the program and had about a year of study and practical experience remaining.

As part of the requirements to complete my certification, I needed to fly by myself for a weekend intensive. This was the first time since the accident that I had to navigate the hectic world of packing for and accomplishing airline travel. Ordinarily this was no problem; I had traveled by myself extensively in the past. In this case, however, without anyone to rely on and with my difficulties with multitasking at the time, I was nervous, anxious, and thought maybe this wasn't a good idea to attempt just yet. It would be up to me to get through the bustling TSA area alone, make sure I had all my carry-on bags, jacket, and shoes, and keep my ticket handy, which can be nerve-wracking for even the most seasoned traveler. Then, I would have to stop and purchase water for the flight, get to the gate, and find my seat.

Luckily, my very dear friend, colleague, and fellow student, Marie, reached out to me and said she would meet my plane, get me to baggage, get on the shuttle, and get us to the ranch. That one act of kindness made all the difference. Peter could get me to the airport and checked in, and Marie would get me to the ranch. All I had to do was get to the gate and board the plane. All would be well.

When we made it to the ranch, everyone was glad to see me, and Melisa and her coaching assistants, Bob and Peggy, made sure I was okay during the long weekend of experiential sessions with the horses.

Midway through the final day of sessions, Melisa invited me to join Bob, Peggy, and her for lunch. To me, this was like being "invited" to the principal's office. From my perspective, being asked to the principal's office was rarely a good thing. In this case, I really wasn't sure. Since I had not participated much during the weekend, I didn't think I'd done anything wrong. And since Melisa never invited any student to join her for lunch, I was definitely curious. Of course, I said yes. During lunch, they asked how I was doing and wanted to know if I needed any help or had any questions. No, I responded, I was doing fine. I'd been really tired at the end of the first day, but I thought I was doing surprisingly well. Then came the real reason they wanted to talk with me.

"So, we have noticed that you haven't stepped up to coach at all this weekend," Bob said.

I was mostly unaware of this but reassured them I was doing well. I explained that I was enjoying the process of taking in everything and learning from others. Bob gently prodded, "Yes, and we have noticed that you haven't stepped up to coach at all this weekend."

I sat back in my chair and gave this some thought. Then I started to tear up and said, "If I don't get in the round pen and partner with the horses, I won't find out that I can't do it anymore." That was a huge revelation for me—both frightening and a very real potential outcome. I had been training to partner with my horses for a year and a half. *What if my brain is so damaged that I won't be able to do this? What if the doctor's prognosis turns out to be true?*

That afternoon, I volunteered to coach. I knew I would have to face the overwhelming possibility that I would not be able to partner with the horse and guide my client through her experience, but I *had* to find out. Just before entering the round pen, I closed my eyes, took a deep breath, and heard a voice, "Don't worry, you've got this." I started the session.

The client told me that she was the caregiver for everyone in her family and was feeling overwhelmed. While she was telling me this, QT, my horse partner for this session, came up behind her and started licking her left hand. She ignored him. I asked her more questions about her caregiving and then turned to questions related to how she took care of her own needs. She said she didn't have time for her own needs. QT continued to lick her left hand. I asked her to put out both of her hands. Then I told her that energetically, we give with our right hand, and we receive with our left hand. QT stood with us, and when she put her hands down, he started licking her left hand once again.

"What do you think he is doing right now?" I asked. She looked at me quizzically. "He has been trying to bring your attention to your receiving energy," I continued. "He is telling you that you need to open up yourself to receive what you need to take care of yourself first. If you don't take care of yourself, you can't fully take care of the others you are responsible for."

She turned, threw her arms around QT, and cried. Then, she thanked me for the session and acknowledged that she had to work on receiving for herself.

We left the round pen, and I received a hug from Bob and congratulations for stepping up. A few minutes later, one of my colleagues came up to me and asked me how I knew what QT was doing. That was a surprise to me because I thought it was obvious what he had been trying to convey. It was also the moment that I knew my brain function had improved significantly in the intuitive requirements needed to partner and understand the wisdom of the horses. I knew to the core of my being that, yes, I absolutely could do this work, and I was still damn good at it. In fact, even better than before the accident. Whatever got "broken" in my head trauma had reweaved itself and become stronger. As a result, I was given the opportunity to rely more and more on my intuition and spiritual connection with the horses for the greatest good of my clients.

CHAPTER 15

Home Sweet Home

Trust in your journey and you will find your paradise.

JANUARY 2011. I had graduated from the equine coaching program, being part of the first graduating class that had begun in January 2009. Armed with my new Equine Gestalt Coaching Method certification, I knew that a public horse boarding facility would not be optimal to the type of work I would be doing with clients.

For instance, if I was working with a horse and client in the facility's round pen and another boarder wanted to use the pen, I would have to leave mid-session with the client. And if the client was experiencing a major breakthrough (or, as is sometimes the case, a breakdown) and other boarders were around, they could certainly stop and watch, and I couldn't ask them not to.

No, a boarding facility was not the place for me to start my Equine Facilitated Success Coaching business. It was time to move out of state and begin again. I was finally recognizing my pattern and ability to see another opportunity and have the courage to act upon it.

Peter's main office headquarters was in New Jersey, and he traveled frequently back and forth across the country. Technically, he worked from home, and it didn't matter where home was, so we put the California house on the market and started looking at ranches we would be able to afford once the house sold.

While I was still participating in the "Touched by a Horse" classes, Peter flew to Colorado and met me on Sundays after the weekend classes ended. We then took Monday and sometimes Tuesday to go ranch shopping. Since having joined the "Touched by a Horse" program and being required to spend eight weekend intensives in Longmont, Colorado, at the TBAH ranch, I'd begun to fall in love with the lifestyle and energy of Colorado. I loved the altitude, clean air, and distinct difference in the ability to be in nature that Colorado offered. In Los Angeles, the landscape consists of house upon house upon house with pockets of concrete jungles. Colorado, with wide open expanses of land and sky, was like night and day from Los Angeles. For me, it represented a slice of heaven.

During our shopping excursions, my realtor, Devon, and I would usually breeze through the main house, look at each other, and say at the same time, "Let's go see the barn." Devon was in the same "Touched by a Horse" certification program as I was, and she was also an experienced horsewoman. She knew exactly what I would need in a self-contained coaching facility. I was grateful we had met and that, as a realtor, she agreed to work with Peter and me to find the perfect ranch for my new business.

After almost a full year on the market, the California house finally sold, and we had less than a month to find a ranch and move. We flew out to Colorado on Memorial Day weekend and saw as many ranches as we could. My head was spinning with all the options. I am thankful that Peter is a wiz with spreadsheets and had designed one that listed all the places we visited—with pros, cons, and in-betweens.

We finally found the perfect place on that Sunday. It was six beautiful acres about twenty minutes from Castle Rock, the nearest town. Every ranch around us was at least five acres, and an added bonus was that the area could not be subdivided. There would be no major housing developments in the foreseeable future. We put in an offer on Memorial Day 2011 and moved to Begin Again Ranch on July 5, 2011. We actually ended up having to rent our California house back for a week to line up escrow closing on the new ranch. Obviously, the name of the ranch, Begin Again Ranch, came from my lifetime of beginning again and again ... over and over. Yet, I had a deep sense of knowing that this would be my final "out of state" move.

The big day for our cross-country move finally arrived. It was time to start the next chapter in our life adventure. Excited to hit the road, yet knowing we were temporarily leaving our horses behind, I made a trip up to the stables and promised Smarty and Bodhi that they would be following us to our new home in a few weeks. This was very important because for months, as I worked with Bodhi in the round pen, he followed me around, and I could hear him distinctly saying, "You're taking me with you, you're taking me with you, you're taking me with you." I assured him on countless occasions that, "Yes, I'm taking you with me, dude. You are part of the family, and I would never leave you behind. You saved my life, and we are energetically connected forever."

I confirmed all the care, feeding, exercise, and transport details with my friend and horse "sitter" at the boarding facility, Kristen, who would be caring for the horses and would be present when the horse transport company, Bob Hubbard Horse Transport, arrived to take them to Colorado in a few weeks. Since Kristen was our go-to horse sitter whenever Peter and I had to be away, she knew my routine and was comfortable with the care, needs, and idiosyncrasies of both Smarty and Bodhi.

Peter and I checked and rechecked the U-Haul trailer we had rented for all our important personal items, as well as twenty bales of California Orchard Hay to have on hand when the horses arrived in Colorado. Knowing that horses' digestive systems are quite fragile, we could not just switch hay. We had to bring California bales with us and would gradually wean them onto the Colorado hay.

We pulled out of the California driveway for the last time, and off we went. It was a rather low-key drive-off. The neighbors weren't out, and friends did not line the sidewalk. There was no big fanfare: no one to say goodbye, no one to see us off, no confetti, and no balloons. I did not feel sad about that, though, and since neither Peter nor I are extreme extroverts, we were comfortable with the understated start of our journey to Colorado. My excitement to partner with my horses on our own property made getting on the road exhilarating.

We headed out Interstate 15 across California and spent the first night in Baker, California. Not nearly as far as we had hoped for the first night, but we had gotten a later start then we had planned.

A few miles into our second day's journey, I looked in the passenger side mirror and noticed smoke coming off the wheel well of the trailer. *Well that can't be good*, I thought. Peter pulled into the first rest stop so we could check it out. Yes, the wheel well was definitely smoking. And with all that hay in the trailer, we were concerned. We took no chances and called AAA for roadside service. Peter explained that it was the U-Haul trailer causing the problem. AAA had to bring a special flatbed truck that just barely fit the U-Haul—part of each wheel was hanging off the trailer. Back we went to Baker. It turned out that U-Haul would have to bring in a new trailer from Victorville, which was almost 100 miles away, and they could not deliver it until the next day.

Other than hosting the world's largest thermometer, there is not much happening in Baker. We were able to find a decent motel (the Wills Fargo Inn) that accepted dogs and spent our second night still stuck in California. A new trailer finally showed up the following day, and in 105-degree heat, we transferred all our important possessions, as well as all the hay, from one trailer to another. Just past midday, we were back on the road. Peter looked over at me and said, "You know we're not going to get as far as we wanted today." And I responded, "I don't care, just get us the hell out of California."

It felt like the state was doing its best to make it difficult for us to leave. I felt like I had to fight for this new opportunity, and after what I had been through with my TBI, obstacles on our road trip were not going to stop me; I'd learned how to fight my way up and out of difficulty. We made it just across the border into St. George, Utah. Thank goodness we were out of state … this time I could say *finally*!

Once we were permanently out of California, I began to relax and enjoy the journey. We'd had to drive through snippets of Nevada and Arizona before crossing into Utah, where we spent the night. This part of the trip was refreshingly unexciting. I found myself getting more and more delighted as we turned on to Interstate 70 and headed into the actual Rocky Mountains. Trees, forests, and mountains have always been my happy place, and as we drove onward, I settled in and thoroughly enjoyed the view, the clear, fresh air, and the anticipation of our new beginning.

The next day would be our very first full day at our new home. Six glorious acres in the front range of the Rocky Mountains. It was a nine-hour straight shot from St. George, Utah, to Sedalia, Colorado. We pulled into our new, unpaved driveway around 9:00 p.m. While unpacking what we would need to be comfortable that first night, I looked up and caught my breath. So many, many stars. I was so very happy and could feel my heart swell and skip a beat as I took in the enormity of the universe. This was the first time I would be living in a place with no light pollution. Even though I had never given it much thought before, I knew that having this much land and sky was immensely important to the healing of my soul. We were HOME.

Begin Again Ranch, Sedalia, Colorado

CHAPTER 16

Reunited

*Wrap yourself in the healing power of animals and
nature. There is nothing more magical.*

ON JULY 11, as the *almost* full moon was rising over the butte, an
eighteen-wheeler came down the main road and stopped outside
the house. Smarty and Bodhi were about to join us on their new
ranch. I had been waiting in breathless anticipation for them to
arrive, knowing that it had been a two-day drive with no stops
for the horses. Smarty and Bodhi were the first delivery on a
cross-country trip the semi was making. When I contracted with
the transport company, I made sure that my horses would be first
off the truck. I was told they would be making one more delivery

after mine ... in North Carolina. I was so excited to show Smarty and Bodhi their new home.

The transport drivers opened the side of the truck and set up a ramp. Then they arranged side boards so the horses could not step off the side. They even put down a carpet so they would not slip. What great service! I was grateful I'd paid to have my babies transported safely and professionally and did not attempt to trailer them ourselves.

Bodhi walked off first. Cool as can be, with not a care in the world. I threw my arms around him and told him how glad I was that he was safely home. I handed him off to Devon, who had come over to be part of the welcome committee, and waited for Smarty. I had asked Devon to be there since I did not know how crazed Smarty and Bodhi might be after two days in a truck, and I knew Peter was not yet comfortable handling high-energy horses.

Now it was Smarty's turn to step out of the truck. Unlike Bodhi, she ran down the ramp all hyped up and ready to get the hell out of the enclosed space. I walked her around a bit until she *sort of* calmed down. Then Devon and I walked both of them down the driveway to the fully enclosed barn.

Each stall—there were three—had a doorway out to a dry paddock. Because Smarty and Bodhi were already used to "being in a box," I had closed the doors to the paddock and put each of them into a stall. I had already laid out fresh shavings, water, and hay and spent time with them as they acclimated to their new "boxes." That night, I left the main barn doors open so they could enjoy the energy of the July full moon.

The next morning, I woke up early and walked down to the barn. It was now my total responsibility to care for, feed, and clean up after Bodhi and Smarty. No more sleeping in, knowing that the barn manager would feed my horses and muck the stalls. It was my first day of waking up at 5:00 a.m. every morning, no matter what the weather, to check on and feed the horses. I portioned out their hay and walked into the stalls to welcome them home again.

That first week, I realized the enormity of the decision we had made to move to a ranch. There was so much to do and learn. Sure, I knew the basics, but now everything would be my responsibility. And until Peter learned and became more comfortable around the horses, I would carry the burden of being *the one* with the most knowledge and expertise. I also knew that I had a lot more to learn too. Until Peter retired, it would be my responsibility to feed the horses, let them out, clean and refill the water buckets, change the shaving, and muck the stalls. Peter took over the mucking on weekends, which was a huge help to me, and gave me a slight break from all the chores.

That first morning, I opened up the stall door to the outdoor runs and latched them open. Both horses were too busy eating to notice, at first. Then, as they got more comfortable that "Mom" was with them and they had their food and water, they began to look around as they chewed and realized there was a big open space outside the back door.

"What is this?" Smarty seemed to say. She took a mouthful of hay, walked over to the door, and looked out. I could see her taking it all in. She came back in for another mouthful and went back to chew in the doorway. She put both front feet out the door and looked around, then stepped back in, because of course she didn't want to get stuck out there when the food and water were inside.

Smarty is very much my cautious one. She likes to check things out slowly, to figure it out and determine whether it is in her best interest to explore. Bodhi, on the other hand, jumps right in and makes his determination as he goes. Before long, they were both standing in the paddock, looking out over the six acres that were now theirs to roam and explore.

My next concern: If I let them out on pasture, would I be able to get them back in? As California horses that had never been on pasture, I did not want them out for too many hours a day. If they ate too much fresh green, sweet grass, it could affect their hooves and cause something called "founder." Founder occurs when there is inflammation of the laminae (folds of tissue connecting the pedal bone to the hoof). When there is inflammation and subsequently degeneration of the laminae (as is seen in an interruption to the blood supply), laminitis results. This can happen if the horse ingests too much sweet grass, and since my horses had never been out on pasture, it was a real possibility.

As I contemplated my choices, I watched as Smarty and Bodhi looked out longingly over the pasture. I knew I had to let them out to "be horses." I opened Smarty's gate first. With that gate open, she now had access to the entire arena pasture (we called it the arena pasture because my full-size riding arena was located there). Smarty stood in her paddock area, not sure what the open gate meant. I called to her and coaxed her to the doorway. Then I stepped back and motioned for her to come out.

As I did that, I had Peter open Bodhi's gate. He definitely waited for Smarty to give him the signal that all was okay. Now that they were no longer in a facility with many other horses, and since they had journeyed together for a few days, Smarty took the lead and embraced her inner alpha mare. In a wild herd, there is always an alpha mare that all the other horses look to for guidance. In my herd of two, Smarty was that lead mare (after me, of course).

As lead mare, she had to determine how the herd (in this case, Bodhi) responded. She realized that I was not going to put a halter on her and lead her someplace. No, this was six acres of pure freedom. She stepped out, looked over at Bodhi, and then she ran, and bucked, and reared, and kicked, and ran some more. He immediately joined in. It was a joy to watch them run and explore because they wanted to, and not because someone was forcing them to run by chasing them with a lunge whip.

Now the magical trick would be to coax them back into their

enclosed paddocks. After letting them stay out for about two hours, it was time to get them in. What to do … what to do? To start, I walked out to where they stood together in the pasture. No halter, no ropes. I just wanted to take a moment and be with them and let them know that all of this land was now their home. I petted them and scratched them. I stood with them for a while and then walked away.

About a half-hour later, I walked out again. This time with a halter. I walked up to Smarty, put on the halter, and walked her back to the gate. Bodhi came with us. *Well that was easy,* I thought. I also had a bucket of yummies for each of them in their respective paddock areas. This was teaching them that when they came in from pasture, there would be a bucket of yummies waiting for them in the paddock. I did this for the first few days, and then one day I just stood in the paddock, opened the gate (which made a loud squeaking sound), and Smarty came running with Bodhi close behind. There would be no more going out to get them. They now came running to me.

It was not long after arriving that I told Peter I wanted to take down the fence that separated Smarty and Bodhi. It was risky because neither one of them had ever shared space with another horse. But I knew it was worth the risk. Smarty and Bodhi knew they were family. Hell, they had traveled halfway across the country together stuck in a moving box. Albeit, a big box, with food, water, and a window, but still a big box. And now they were Lord and Lady of six acres. I knew they would not fight over the shared space, as long as Bodhi knew that Smarty was in charge.

We removed the panels while they were out on pasture, since we did not want their "help" as we struggled to carry the panels out of the paddock. (Okay, as I struggled. For Peter, it was no problem. I, on the other hand, needed to literally hold up my end of a more-than-seventy-pound steel panel—not an easy feat for someone who is 5 feet 4 inches tall!) Once we were done, when I brought in the horses, I did so using the individual paddock gates they were used to, even though they would end up in the same larger paddock.

Smarty came in her gate and went right up to her yummy bucket, and Bodhi came in his gate and went to his yummy bucket, which contained a mash of shredded beet pulp with molasses and rolled oats mixed with water. (Now doesn't that sound delicious? Apparently to a horse, it's like high-end truffles.) After devouring the yummies, Smarty looked up and realized she could now walk over to where Bodhi was standing. She walked over to him, but he kept eating and was not at all concerned with having another horse near him while he ate. He didn't display any increase of energy or "pissy ears." Instead, he remained calm and unaffected.

Pissy ears is when a horse pins its ears down close to its head to indicate either "I'm really mad" or "You better move." The lead mare uses "pissy ears" as a first warning to others in the herd, and if they don't "listen," then that's when things can escalate. Smarty had tried it with me once or twice, but I immediately put her in her place and established that I am the lead mare.

In this case, there was no kerfuffle. All was well, and they've been together ever since.

Not long after we arrived and settled in, my colleague, Marie, asked if she could board her horse, Misty, with us in the empty stall. Since Marie and I both offered the same equine coaching services, it seemed like a good fit. The biggest consideration was that we would need to coordinate our client schedules so we didn't overlap each other. One of my selling points is that when you as a client are here for a session, there is no one or nothing else happening on the ranch at the same time. This is your private experience with me and the horses.

Misty was a fine addition to the herd, and now Bodhi, the only male, had his own harem to lord over. It was heartening to watch as Bodhi went from a sad, broken horse who frequently stood with his head hanging down, to a confident leader of the herd, with his head up and eyes bright. He was fulfilled in his role as main protector and top dude. I was thrilled to see him emerge from the funk he'd remained in after participating in my TBI, even though I told him frequently that it was not his fault and that he'd actually saved my life by refusing to go out on the trail that fateful day.

After Misty arrived and was settled in, Marie asked if I would take in another boarder. Her friend's horse, Captain, was at the same facility where Misty had been boarded. Marie partnered with Captain in her client work and felt it would be great for her and Captain if he was with Misty at Begin Again Ranch. All of a sudden, I was caregiver to four horses. I went from occasional daily care with horses off-property in California to 24/7 care of four horses in Colorado—a big learning curve and a huge time commitment. I loved it and still do.

Unfortunately, Bodhi was not happy to have another guy around. He really liked being Head Dude and was not going to give that up. Captain was also an alpha male and was not going to back down without a fight, so he and Bodhi did not get along, no matter how long I took to acclimate them to each other. I had to split up the boys in two different pastures and rotated the girls each day. Ultimately, it all worked out.

Smarty, Me & Bodhi

CHAPTER 17

Equine Coaching

*Accept all the help that is offered; most likely
it is a gift from Spirit.*

WHILE THE HORSES were getting more comfortable being on a ranch, it was time for me to step up and start networking. As a high introvert, walking into a roomful of people I don't know is the worst thing I can think of doing. But if I was to get my name and services out there, I had to do it.

My first foray into "networking land" was with a monthly group called Camp Experience. It was an all-women group, and I knew women were my key demographic. Yet, the need to network in order to gain potential clients was a whole new world for me and quite different from holding a position in a corporate environment and supporting a high-level executive. As sole owner, CEO, and the only employee of Begin Again Ranch, if I didn't do it, it didn't get done. *Whew! No pressure.*

The first thing I discovered when I chatted with other women was that they had no idea what I did with horses. That was to be expected, though, since I was part of a very young methodology and a member of the first certification class for equine gestalt coaching. I found that when I tried to explain how I and the horses worked together, their eyes would glaze over, and they would say, "I'm sorry, you do *what* with horses?"

Frustrating, yes. But I also took it as an opportunity to educate people on an alternative form of therapy. I realized that there are many people who do not wish to sit in a therapist's office and talk. So, I positioned myself and my services as an alternative to talk therapy by pointing out that an individual comes out to the ranch to partner with horses and have an opportunity to work through blocks in their lives and aspects of living that might not be working the way they'd like.

Still, it was challenging. When I was "chief of staff" at The Walt Disney Company, it was part of my unwritten job description to protect and promote my boss. Not me, but my boss. Promoting *me* was an enigma. I truly did not even know how to start doing that. Having to talk about myself and promote Begin Again Ranch was a whole new ballgame. I was certainly not comfortable. I did it anyway. Yes, I made mistakes. Yes, it was painful for me. And yes, I kept at it.

One year in particular, my New Year's resolution was to attend every networking meeting I could, even if that meant three meetings per week. That resolution was extremely difficult for me, as putting myself willingly into group settings was not my forte. I hated it, and at that stage in my life, it had been years since I drank to take the edge off before I attended a social or, in this case, a professional event. I was stone cold sober and had to rely on my individual worthiness to succeed. But I did it.

I joined four or five groups, some at a significant annual membership fee. They were usually held at a restaurant where we were strongly encouraged to buy lunch. Although I was spending a significant amount of money to connect with others, my thought was to keep doing it so I could meet as many people as possible to get my message out there. The mistake was that most of these meetings were not comprised of my demographic (women struggling with "Is this all there is?" syndrome). Instead, the groups consisted of women trying to sell their products. For me, these events were draining, sometimes exhausting, and rarely, if ever, did I "close a sale" and gain a client. This process also went against everything my introverted, highly intuitive, and empathic self thrived on.

Halfway through the year, I gave myself permission to stop attending the meetings that didn't feel good. I started to weed out the groups that were not my demographic. I began to listen to my intuition, even when I was not with the horses. Talk about having an aha moment! I found that the groups I did attend were more about building meaningful relationships and not focused on a hard sell, "buy my widgets" approach. I pared it down to one or two meaningful groups each month and attended as many of their social and business-building events as I could. The most important thing I learned was that it did not matter how many networking groups I belonged to. What mattered was how many true relationships I built—something that was still truly challenging for me.

Since those early days of establishing my business, I have learned the lesson of being my true and authentic self. Now I belong to only one networking group, Polka Dot Powerhouse, a national organization with chapters in every state, exclusively female, whose goal is to empower and support every member—a much better way for me to connect with others.

Something I learned a few years later through my Jack Canfield training (more about this in the next chapter) was E+R=O. The Event + your Response = your Outcome. Just like my TBI, I could have curled up in a ball and hid in my office at home. That would have been one response. Instead, my response was to take each setback or uncomfortable event as a learning experience. As a result, my outcome has been a successful equine-facilitated coaching business.

One thing I will admit here is that I do not recommend anyone move to a new state where you don't know anyone and do not have a "built-in" support system and potential clients to pull from. Starting over has been my MO and a definite pattern during my lifetime, yet it doesn't necessarily make life easier. In fact, I am still trying to determine the exact reason, message, or lesson for me to learn about my past need to begin again, most especially so that I do not need to continue doing it.

Early on, when I first started networking, I wish I had figured out that instead of meeting with potential referral partners or clients over coffee, people would have benefitted from an invitation out to the ranch. The experience would have helped them understand what I did, and I might have gained more clients sooner. Eventually, I caught on to how to offer such an opportunity. I called it a "complimentary horse experience." By doing so, they could experience partnering with the horses firsthand and get a better understanding of my services and how I differed from a traditional talk therapist.

One of my first demonstration events was for my leads group through the Castle Rock Chamber of Commerce. After completing my insurance-required safety demo, I asked for a volunteer. Patty immediately put her hand up, and I invited her into the round pen with Smarty and me. As I started to ask Patty some basic coaching questions, I kept my eyes on her body language and what Smarty was doing. Patty said she really didn't have any issues to bring to the experience; she just wanted to experience being with a horse.

Since I knew Patty from our group, I knew that was not completely true. Yet, because I was facilitating a demo group, it was certainly not appropriate to invite Patty to explore her statement in front of everyone. Instead, I invited Patty to go up to Smarty and start talking with her as if she were a potential client. As Patty approached, Smarty turned her rump to her and walked away. I told Patty to keep trying.

"Your horse doesn't like me," she said.

"How can you know that? You haven't even tried to make a connection with her. Please try again," I responded.

The same thing happened. I walked over to Patty and asked her, "Do you expect her to bond with you immediately?" Although Patty did not respond, from what I'd observed in our group, I believed that as a bubbly extrovert, she did indeed expect people to be drawn to her. I suspected that she rarely had to approach people. They came to her, like moths to a flame. The fact that Smarty ignored her was a new experience for Patty, and I could see she didn't know what to do. As she stood there, I asked her whether she ever approached people who did not come up to her first when she was in a networking environment, and she replied, "No."

I went on, "Just think about how many potential clients you are missing out on because you don't approach others and engage them in conversation. Do you want to try again with Smarty?"

She agreed to give it another go. I coached her to take a deep breath, then approach Smarty as if she were someone Patty wanted to meet and get to know. She took in the advice, inhaled deeply, and walked over to Smarty. Then she began to talk to Smarty as someone Patty wanted to learn more about. Smarty did not walk away or turn away. Instead, she stood looking at Patty and listening to every word. Patty was able to pet Smarty and make a connection with a new, potential client. Patty's session gave her an insight as to how many opportunities she was missing out on just because she expected people to come to her.

I traded out horses, and Bodhi joined me in the round pen. I asked for another volunteer, and Steve raised his hand, albeit rather reluctantly. He joined Bodhi and me in the pen. Bodhi had been standing quietly, nuzzling the ground and looking for grass or something to eat. As soon as Steve joined me in the middle of the pen, Bodhi started running around. With his energy high, Bodhi cut right near us. Then he kicked out and reared up, which was very unlike Bodhi. I knew something was up, and Bodhi knew Steve was the client. Luckily, Steve did not freak out. I had him start to take control of Bodhi's high energy by "telling" Bodhi to run in a circle; Bodhi could stop when Steve gave him permission to stop. After a few minutes, Bodhi's energy leveled out, and we let him stop running.

As Steve and I debriefed, Bodhi calmly walked over, put

his nose on Steve's shoulder, and joined us. A few of the other participants were concerned with Bodhi's energy and wanted to know what was going on. Since this was a demo for a group, and not a private session, I was not going to go too deep into what I knew was happening. Instead, I responded, "Well, it's a guy thing. Bodhi has big energy. Steve has big energy. And Bodhi was testing Steve to see who would be in charge. At the end, when Bodhi came over and joined us, he was saying, "Okay, I'll let you think you're in charge. Let's be friends."

After my demonstrations, I returned Bodhi to his stall and caught Steve alone. Since we'd gotten to know each other through the group, I felt comfortable to share with him what I'd observed. "I know you must have gone through some serious stuff as a Navy Seal," I offered. "When Bodhi started running around as soon as you entered the pen, what that told me is that you have a lot of emotions just below the surface that may be ready to explode. I would much rather have you explode here on the ranch and not on the playground with your daughters. Just think about it. I'm here if you ever want to explore those emotions." I was concerned enough to bring this to his attention, knowing, however, that what he would do with the information I offered was entirely up to him.

In a demo situation such as this, if something significant presents itself during a volunteer session, and if I have the opportunity to speak with the individual alone after the session, I do so. In that way, I respect their privacy while letting them know that the horses and I can help them deal with and explore the obstacle or challenge they may have buried.

In June 2014, I found myself with an empty stall. Captain and Misty had passed on and Marie moved her new horse, Mariah, closer to where she was now living. I wasn't actively looking to fill the stall, but Spirit delivers messages and partners when we need them. In this case, his name was Ki, and he was a black Missouri Fox Trotter.

His "mom," Barbara, had decided to continue her shamanic journey and was moving to Ecuador. Ki needed a new home. Barbara had heard about the type of work I was doing with clients and asked if I would be interested in meeting Ki. As a result, Ki joined our family and, for the most part, fit in well.

However, because he was a boy, Bodhi once again did not appreciate Ki and certainly did not welcome him with open hooves. Whenever they were out on pasture, which was every day, Bodhi chased Ki all around God's green acres, and Ki did his best to stay out of Bodhi's way. Unfortunately, Ki is very sensitive. Great for client work, but not so great for his tummy. He soon developed an ulcer. We took care of him immediately, and with proper medication, he is healthy and one of my best client partners.

One of my first individual clients was a lovely lady named Julie. Julie had become engaged, and only a few months into the engagement, her fiancé, Walt, passed away in front of her. As she was going through Walt's things and helping his family clean up, she came across my brochure. Neither one of us knew why Walt had my brochure, nor where he might have gotten it. Again, I firmly believe that there are no coincidences—Spirit sends us messages, and it is up to us to become aware of them. This was no coincidence.

The horses and I worked with Julie for three sessions, focusing on her grief and loss. Not long after Julie completed her sessions, she was presented with a diagnosis of multiple sclerosis. She came out to see the horses and get help processing this new life challenge she would need to navigate.

One of the symptoms of MS can be difficulty with balance and coordination. I had Julie enter the round pen with Ki and asked her to walk around, as I wanted to assess her balance before we got started. As she walked around, Ki stayed with her. When they got to a section of the pen that was muddy from rain, Ki slowed down, lowered his head, and Julie grabbed on to his mane to steady herself through the mud.

When she got on solid ground, I stopped her and asked, "What happened there with Ki?"

"He was taking good care of me and made sure I didn't slip in the mud," she responded.

"How did you feel?" I inquired.

"Safe and supported," she said with a smile on her face.

"Okay, keep going please."

She and Ki started to walk again. Before they got anywhere near the mud, Ki stepped in front of her and stopped her forward momentum.

"Is this the same thing as before?" I asked.

"No, this is different."

"Is he stopping you from moving forward?"

"Yes, he is."

I gave her a moment to think about that and then asked, "What are you telling yourself about your MS diagnosis that is keeping you from moving forward in your life?"

I could see her start to tear up, and she almost whispered, "That's exactly what I'm doing."

The connection with Ki gave her the strength and support she needed to admit she was scared and holding herself back from moving past the diagnosis to continue to live a full and productive life, whatever that might look like in the future.

In coaching, I never run to the client to offer a hug or deliver a tissue. That would immediately interrupt the processing needed to get past an issue or challenge. Tears are a major part of the process, so it's important for me to let them flow. In this session with Julie, I allowed her to be with her emotions.

After a few minutes, I asked, "Are you going to let this diagnosis keep you from living the best life you can?"

Julie paused a moment, took a deep breath, and said, "No, I'm not."

"And what are you going to do about it?"

She put both hands on Ki, pushed him out of the way, and started walking. I stood outside the pen and did an internal happy dance. After a few steps, Ki joined her at her side, and they walked around the pen together. He was with her to be supportive and encouraging whenever she needed him, just as others would be there to support Julie as she moved forward in her life.

One thing I had feared as I began to build my business was that my TBI would have a negative effect on my ability to work with my horses. As I worked with more and more clients, I came to find out that my intuition and connection with the messages from my horse partners was stronger than it ever had been. Whatever part of my brain that had been "broken" enabled the opportunity for my new neural pathways to engage in a deeper ability to intuit what the horses were trying to impart to my clients.

On one occasion, I was facilitating a complimentary horse experience. Donna, my potential client, and I were standing in the round pen with Smarty as her partner. She was telling me about herself. During an initial meeting, a client usually shares preliminary background information, and I am able to pick up what is really going on with them, which comes more from what they are *not* telling me.

At one point, Smarty, who was meandering around as we chatted, moved up behind Donna and started backing into her. Donna was unaware that this 1,100-pound horse's butt was right behind her. I interrupted Donna and asked, "How are things going at home?" She was taken aback and asked, "What do you mean?" I explained that Smarty's butt was right behind her, which told me there was a possibility that her root chakra needed balancing.

The root chakra is located at the base of our spine and buttocks and represents our foundation, stability, and basic safety needs. Because Smarty backed her powerful, stable root chakra into Donna, I intuitively knew to ask about her home life. Donna admitted that she and her husband were having trouble and were talking about separation. She didn't know how to share that with her kids. It turned out that *this* was the real issue Donna needed to work on during our session. And, for me, it was another moment of gratitude for the heightened intuition and connection to my horse partners that came from my TBI accident.

Since 2011, I have continued to partner with my horses to bring information to my clients. My horses know when we're with a client, and they begin to work immediately. No matter what the horse is doing, or not doing, it always has something to do with the needs of the client. It is up to me to then interpret the messages and wisdom of the horses.

Polka Dot Powerhouse – Highlands Ranch Team Building

CHAPTER 18

Something's Missing

Step through the horse shit and keep on moving forward.

AS I STARTED BUILDING MY NEW BUSINESS, I was searching for that magic pill that would propel my business to the next level. Add that issue to the writing on my childhood whiteboard that I was not good enough in my own right, but I could buy my way into community, friendship, and more. I did not have a great recipe for entrepreneurial business success.

Yes, I was doing okay. Yes, I had clients. Yes, I attended networking group meetings regularly. But something was missing. And I was still searching for that missing magical ingredient.

I tried many different options that would lead me to business success. Thinking that certain programs might be the answer, I bought online courses and followed them as best I could, but not religiously. There always seemed to be parts of the course that either did not speak to me or, worse, made me feel uncomfortable.

Then, I hired a sales coach. *Of course, that must be my missing piece.* I worked with Cheryl for more than a year. I really enjoyed our forty-five-minute Zoom calls three times per month, and she gave me many important sales tools and learning opportunities, yet I still hadn't found the magic formula that would lead to a continuous stream of clients.

As I continued to look for the magic pill that would draw clients to me like flies (and I had plenty of flies in the barn, so I knew what that was like), I researched names and groups suggested to me, such as Tony Robbins and Thrive Academy, but I found that many of the experts were so over-the-top rah-rah and extremely high energy that I immediately knew their delivery method would never resonate with me. I feared I would never find someone who resonated with my vibration. But I kept searching.

For some reason, I'd been receiving email invitations and Facebook posts from someone named Jack Canfield. I didn't know why I started receiving those emails and posts, but I did know there are no coincidences. I still thank Spirit today for introducing me to Jack. Jack is an older gentleman with a lower energetic delivery, and yet profoundly wise. *Oh my goodness, finally, someone whose message delivery matches my energetic vibration.* I watched his YouTube videos and bought and devoured his books (Jack is the co-author of the mega successful *Chicken Soup for the Soul* series and my favorite book, *The Success Principles*). Everything he taught gave me validation for the way I had lived my life over the years. I had never known there were actual "rules" or "principles" to follow. And now I did.

I attended Jack's weeklong *Breakthrough to Success* program held annually in Scottsdale, Arizona, and the following year, I was chosen to be on Jack's assistant team. I considered that a great honor—I would be able to participate not only in the daylong teachings but also in all of the "behind the scenes" activities necessary to put on a training event for three hundred people. It was during this event that I considered "upgrading" my current training with Jack to sign up for his live program. This was not an easy decision. It was a huge time commitment, plus it was a very large financial investment. Not only would I have to pay for the course itself, but I would also have to fly out and stay for a week at a hotel in Newport Beach and then again in Los Angeles.

Every morning while in Scottsdale, I woke up early, dressed for my exercise, tied up my sneakers, and headed out for a power walk around the property. I'd learned that the hotel had an enclosure that housed a giant desert tortoise named Cecil. I'd found the enclosure on previous walks but had never seen Cecil. On this last morning of the event, I planned to do a walking meditation focused on whether I should join Jack's live teaching program.

Every other morning, I'd left my room and headed directly onto the walkways around the resort. On this final morning, I distinctly heard a voice say, "Go left." Since I have always been one to listen to divine messages, of course I went left. Listening to my power playlist, I picked up the pace. As I neared the end of my walk, I knew I was approaching Cecil's enclosure. Much to my surprise, there he was. Right up near the fence. Apparently, he was waiting for me.

I took this picture and showed it to one of the other assistants before the program started. As I did, Patty Aubrey, the president of Jack's company, looked over my shoulder, and said, "Did you know that Jack's totem animal is a tortoise?" and walked on. *Wow, was Cecil a message that I needed to continue my training*

with Jack? You might think that seeing Cecil on the morning I needed to decide if I was going to take Jack's live training was just a coincidence, but in my world, there are no coincidences. I signed up and found out that as a bonus, I would receive a taped testimonial from Jack about my business and programs after I completed my training.

Upon completing my certification, I added many more tools to my ever-expanding toolbox, including transformational speaking. Jack has acknowledged me as his first equine-facilitated success coach, and I have incorporated all of Jack's teachings in my own *Begin Again Breakthrough Strategies* program.

Speaking onstage at the Jack Canfield event

As a newly minted transformational speaker, I was booked to give a presentation for Dress for Success Denver and had worked diligently on my PowerPoint presentation. Still not comfortable talking about myself, I struggled with my opening line and introduction. As I sat in my office with my document open and stared blankly at the screen, I thought of a recent introduction I had to present onstage at my Canfield methodology training. I got goosies (goosebumps on my arms, sometimes also referred to as Angel Kisses) as I recalled it.

I knew I had to open with the same vulnerability I'd displayed at the Canfield event. I chose a part of my life that I didn't reveal very often, if at all. "Hi, my name is Terri and I'm an alcoholic. Now I realize that is not usually how to introduce yourself at a non-twelve-step type gathering, but I am an alcoholic and I'm happy to share that I am twenty-one years sober."

While practicing my speech, Peter questioned the opening. He asked, "Do you really want to open with that? You're really putting yourself out there, and it's not an AA meeting or anything." I gave it more thought and felt strongly that it definitely was the way I needed to open. Yes, I needed to open with being vulnerable. I would be talking to a group of women who had or were struggling with life challenges, and I wanted to make sure they knew that my life had not been all peaches and cream.

On the evening of the event, I arrived early and set up my speaker table with giveaways: a flyer for the special DFS women's workshop I was offering and other Begin Again Ranch information. After the conclusion of my speech, after all the attendees who were waiting in line to talk with me had come through (that experience was new and exciting), Gloria, the person at Dress for Success who had booked my appearance, came up to me and said, "I am so glad you opened your presentation the way you did. Did you see the four women who came just before you started and sat at a back table? Well, they are all struggling with alcoholism and had this preconception that "professional speakers" are highly educated, privileged people who have no idea what it's like to struggle with an addiction, and you just proved them wrong."

I was so happy I trusted my intuition and opened with the acknowledgment of my own addiction. That introduction laid my vulnerability on the stage.

Incorporating the Canfield Success Principles into my *Begin Again Breakthrough Strategies* program, I never gave any thought as to how I was going to teach the horses what the success principles were, but I found out quickly that they already knew and had been waiting for me to catch up.

I was working with Bernadette and Alan for couples coaching. On this particular day, they must have had a "discussion" in the car on the way to the ranch, as they were both clearly agitated when they arrived. We were seated in the arena, and I had Bodhi and Ki with us for their session.

"So, what's going on?" I asked.

Alan started talking about what had happened in the car. As he talked, I noticed that Bernadette crossed her legs and her arms and then leaned over. I recognized a classic defensive posture. By this point, Alan was standing up.

I sat there contemplating how I would bring in the first success principle: E+R=O (Event + Response = Outcome). As Alan continued to try and get his point across, I knew this dynamic was a familiar one for them. I considered whether I should start with Alan and change his response, thereby getting a different outcome, or work with Bernadette to change her response.

While I contemplated which way to go, Bodhi joined us, walked in between Bernadette and Alan, grabbed Bernadette's shoelaces, shook her foot, dropped it, and walked off. Bodhi changed Bernadette's response and provided me with the perfect opening to coach them through the process of becoming aware of the event, their response, and what they had to do to change the usual outcome.

I turned toward Bernadette and asked her, "What just happened?"

She responded that Bodhi had shaken her foot and made her shift her focus. I pointed out that she had changed her posture as well. I coached her through Bodhi's lesson by asking her about her focus and posture before Bodhi shook her foot, and she responded that she was focused intently on what Alan was saying, which was something she did whenever they were in the midst of a serious discussion.

"How else might your whole demeanor be interpreted?"

She looked at me slightly perplexed. I knew she didn't recognize what I was pointing out. I said, "With you sitting there, legs and arms crossed, and leaning forward, might it give someone the impression that you are in a protective, defensive mode?"

She sat back, taking in what I had just pointed out. "Wow, I never thought of it that way before."

"How might you change your dynamic in these situations?" I prompted.

She thought about it for a moment, did a whole-body shake, planted her feet on the ground, and placed her hands in her lap.

I turned to Alan. "Now how does that feel for you?"

"So much better," he answered.

I asked them to start again. Alan sat down, Bernadette sat across from him, open and receptive, and they were able to discuss the issue calmly, ultimately reaching an amicable conclusion. By changing their response, they were able to reach the outcome they both wanted.

As I continued to enjoy working and supporting my clients, partnering with my horses, and truly loving life on the ranch, businesswise, it seemed I was still searching for that magic pill. Or was I? Was it a magic pill or something else I was searching for?

The pattern over the course of my life had been the ongoing desire to belong, to have friends, to be accepted. And each time in my life when I realized that I did not belong, nor would I, it was time to move to another city or state, start over, and begin again. Yes, it was usually a clean slate, but boy, was I bringing along a whole heap of major baggage with me. Apparently, I was not yet done with this lesson.

There I was, sitting in a hotel conference room on the last morning of a business presentation. I was an attendee and, of course, on this last morning, it was my *last* opportunity to join the up-level offering. The morning presentation started with insight from current members of this fabulous club. They talked about how they could not have gotten where they were in their business without joining this wonderful club and how amazingly generous it was that (insert name here) was offering this special opportunity to us.

Now all of that may have been true, and many times in the past, I immediately joined. Yes, I'd heard it all before. And yes, I'd pulled out my credit card because I was missing that one *absolutely necessary magic nugget* that would explain to the *muggles of the world* how amazing I was and that they should all be clamoring to work with me. The problem on this particular morning was that at the end of the previous year, I had given myself permission to *stop buying new business webinars and programs* and, instead, chill with the information I had already purchased. I could give my credit card a break too. I reminded myself that I was still paying off my last certification, so why was I considering this new "opportunity"?

And then it hit me. Like a bolt of inspiration—or more like a holy crap!—I realized I was considering the program because I was looking to buy my way into another community of what I hoped were like-minded people. It never occurred to me in the past that belonging was what I was trying to achieve. But it did explain a lot about my past patterns. *Wow!* That realization was a true eye-opener. It was freeing to "label" my patterns, and it was also extremely painful to realize how little I valued myself. It begged the question: When did that limiting belief start?

After getting back to my hotel room and contemplating this question, I remembered all the ways I'd tried to "buy" my way into a group or a relationship. Hadn't I tried to buy my way into spending time with my sister and her girlfriend by paying for a tank of gas for the boat? Hadn't I lost relationships in grammar school and high school because I didn't seem to have the right currency to buy my way in? Hadn't the unspoken message been that a relationship with me was not worth it by itself? And hadn't my inclusion at Disney and my enjoyment of the perks there only existed while I was a cast member, during the time I worked for an officer of the company?

These were powerful life lessons that I had taken with me on this life journey. Something I'd done over and over again with the same results: no lasting community, no lasting relationships. No matter how many times I thought I was erasing the messages on my personal whiteboard, they were still there. Just below the surface.

In light of this revelation, as painful as it was to acknowledge, I did not sign up for this up-level program, and I gave myself permission to stop buying classes and certifications in order to be part of a community. It certainly wasn't worth the financial investment that did not result in any lasting relationships. It was time to take a step back, breathe deep, and finally admit to myself that purchasing inclusion was not working. It was time to rewrite more messages on my personal whiteboard.

CHAPTER 19

My Whiteboard

*I choose to color my life with multiple
shades of gratitude.*

NO MATTER WHO WE BECOME or what we accomplish, we still feel that we're essentially the kid we were at some simpler time long ago. I know that for me, every time I was with my dad, even in my sixties, I became a twelve-year-old. Those early messages written on my personal whiteboard resurfaced as soon as I was in his presence.

My dad passed barely three months ago. He was ninety-three and transitioned from this life relatively peacefully, which is what I had been praying for. While I am still processing his passing and getting used to the new paradigm of not calling him twice a week and never seeing him again, I am taking the time to wonder if there will still be life occurrences when I revert to my twelve-year-old self.

My dad, Ray Cook, was a hardworking provider and a loving husband and father. He did what was expected of him and lived a long and contented life. Yet, he was rarely overly demonstrative or quick with a hug or soothing words. I know he did the absolute best he could, utilizing his own upbringing and being unknowingly influenced by the messages written on the whiteboard of his own life many decades earlier.

Just as they did for my dad, I know that the messages I received growing up have traveled with me my entire life. Somehow that's the trick to success: to learn what those early messages were. We need to embrace them, understand them, and then decide which messages to remove from our personal whiteboard (with bleach and a steel wool pad if we have to) in order to be our true selves, and in order to get to our soul's message—our true purpose.

After surviving the traumatic event of my brain injury, I took that opportunity during my lengthy recovery time to open myself to Spirit and listen to my primary question of why I stayed on this planet. What were the lessons and messages that I disregarded over the course of my life that I needed to pay attention to now? Most important, where did I want to go from here? And, although I was well aware of the negative messages written on my whiteboard, I needed to consider the positive messages that got overlooked or covered up during the course of my life. I actually had to call a few close friends and family members and ask them to share with me a positive strength of mine. Here is what I learned:

I am a loving, supportive, and amazing wife and partner. I am a loyal and supportive friend. I am extremely creative. I almost always look at the bright side of situations. I am a brilliant coach. It is instinctive for me to know exactly what questions or suggestions the client needs to help them process and move beyond their challenges. I am an awesome animal intuitive. I am organized, resilient, and I don't obsess over what others think of me. Wow! Who knew? Certainly not I, that is, not until I asked. These are the most important messages that were written on my personal whiteboard, and yet I'd completely missed them.

There were many messages written on my personal whiteboard that had been unknowingly rewritten by me time and time again, adding to my negative self-image. For instance, during my formative years, it was certainly not the intent of my sister to write on my whiteboard, "You're not worth being part of my community unless you pay your way in." And yet that is the message I took with me through much of my life. I'm sure she just wanted her space and did not want her little sister tagging along every day. After all, we shared a room at home and on vacations, we went to the same school, and she was at the age where she was testing her individuality and her wings. I get that now, but I didn't at the time, as I viewed that message through my lens of "not worth it."

As much as I now have the awareness to focus on my strengths and positive attributes, I look at the messages on my whiteboard as opportunities for learning. They allow me to search for and find my true purpose in spite of those perceived messages. Looking back over the course of my life journey, I can now say I have more clarity. And I have expertise, knowledge, and experience to share with and offer to my clients as well.

For over a decade, I had the incredible opportunity to work at the top of the Disney Castle. It was an awesome experience, dealing with many different executive personalities. I learned many life lessons at Disney and, most importantly, I knew when it was time for me to walk away from the large, stable salary and the many corporate perks to pursue new adventures. And, if that decision wasn't difficult enough, Spirit gave me the added "opportunity" of my TBI experience to slow down, search deep within, and find my true soul purpose.

Long before my TBI, I'd been "programmed" to believe that working meant working in a corporate office for someone else. Grinding day after day to make sure the boss or the company or the organization was continuing to be successful. With my departure from the corporate and legal worlds, I began to explore other directions, moving toward the healing arts and working with horses. Through those experiences, I started to discover some of my inherent gifts, including my intuition and ability to communicate with animals. After my TBI, suddenly unsure about my future, I needed to look within myself, accept my new "normal," and make the best of my situation. I found the strength—that each one of us is born with—to choose to ignore what the "experts" said my life would look like after my TBI. Instead, I made the decision to push forward and continue on the path that I'd begun prior to my accident.

My head injury was a necessary step in my life's journey to work with horses to heal humans. I was able to look at the event of my TBI as an opportunity to expand my spirituality and embrace my soul purpose for staying on the planet. This realization eased into my consciousness gradually. The more I worked with my horses, the more I became conscious of my ever-expanding ability to interpret the messages from them. This capability became the basis of my equine coaching business.

Starting over at Begin Again Ranch has been the most difficult and the most rewarding chapter of my life thus far. Every day, I get to work with women and couples who are going through their own transformation and support them as they explore their own soul purpose. There have been many business ups and downs over the past several years, and I have gained valuable understanding, patience, maturity, and compassion every step of the way.

There also have been times when I wanted to give up and shut things down. During those times, I remember to be compassionate with myself too. I turn off for a few days, reevaluate the current challenge, and ask myself these extremely important questions: "What story am I telling myself about this situation? What story can I change it to that reflects the reality of this situation? What do I need to do or say to make that change and write a new message for myself?"

We all make up stories about the issues, challenges, or situations we are faced with. It is human nature. Especially if we don't have, or allow ourselves to "see," all of the information. As human beings, we are compelled to fill in the blanks. My "go to" story was that I was not good enough, or worthy enough, to _____. I filled in the blank with whatever would keep my storyline going. Recovering from a TBI gave me the opportunity to change my ongoing story to: "Well, that was different. How can I learn from *that* and make it better next time?"

Because of my injury and my horses, whose lives depend on always living in the present, I, too, have come to value living in the present moment. It's an important life lesson that I have come to embrace. This knowledge is also tremendously helpful when I work with clients.

The gift of my brain injury has been the ability to be curious and see the joy in everyday occurrences. Because I am able to work with horses on a daily basis, I find that I smile a whole lot more, I have confidence in myself, and I believe that my equine coaching business is where my passion and joy lie. I get to assist horses in their healing of humans. Everyone benefits.

Each and every day, I get an opportunity to respond to something instead of reacting to it. When something occurs, I take a deep breath, acknowledge what has happened, allow the initial reactive emotions to reveal themselves, and choose to respond with love, calmness, and curiosity. This was a huge life lesson for me, and I am grateful for that enlightenment every day.

Today, I continue to enjoy riding and partnering with my horses to work with clients. Together we are well and happy. My new mantra whenever I hit a speed bump in my path is: Pause, close your eyes, take a deep breath, smile, and … begin again!

I once saw a license plate holder while traveling in Florida that said: "Is there life after Disney." Today, I can tell you unequivocally that the answer is "Yes!" What I have come to know is you don't have to live in the Magic Kingdom to connect with your own magic. Today, far away from the Magic Kingdom, as I take in the immensity of Spirit's gifts, including my deepened intuition and ability to communicate with my animals, I've connected with the magic in my life. And, for the most part, I have erased my original whiteboard story and continue to write and rewrite new messages that include: "I am strong. I am valuable. I have wisdom to share. I AM WORTH IT."

What is the story that you have been telling yourself, and how can you begin to change it? It's never too late to begin again!

A SPECIAL NOTE TO YOU, THE READER

Embrace the audacity of success.

AS AN EQUINE COACH, I support my clients first by listening to what they need to share. Usually, my initial question is: "What is the story you are telling yourself about that issue?" That one question opens up a treasure trove of information for me:

- to explore with them,
- to help them find where it started,
- to identify the message written on their whiteboard,
- and by partnering with the horses, to erase the message with bleach and a steel wool pad.

Only then can we move on to bring clarity and understanding of their own soul purpose.

In addition to my favorite "What story are you telling yourself?" question, I frequently introduce the E+R=O formula: Event + Response = Outcome, the first success principle I learned during my Canfield Methodology Training, and one I teach during my *Begin Again Breakthrough Strategies* program. That formula, with the help of my horses, has helped so many of my clients see messages and patterns that haven't been serving them and begin to make changes to break through to incredible possibilities. Spirit presented me the learning opportunities to connect to my own gifts, and I have immense gratitude for the true magical lessons I have experienced over the course of my life.

The journey toward fulfilling your purpose can be a life-changing adventure. It is possible to learn how to identify and acknowledge, and embrace or reject, the messages written on your personal whiteboard. And it is possible to move forward with an all-encompassing, complete, and breathtaking sense of self and soul purpose.

If you find yourself struggling to gain clarity about your soul purpose or need help identifying, erasing, and rewriting those whiteboard messages, I invite you to contact me. Whether you live in the Denver area or somewhere else in the world, I offer my *Begin Again Breakthrough Strategies* program at Begin Again Ranch. I am available for in-person, one-on-one equine sessions and VIP weekend retreats with my herd of wisdom horses, as well as via Zoom for individual coaching sessions if you can't make it to the ranch. I can be reached through my website: BeginAgainRanch.com or at terri@BeginAgainRanch.com.

In parting, always remember:

No matter what you've been through or are going through, it is your choice to close your eyes, take a deep breath, smile, and Begin Again.

Wishing you love, joy, clarity, and purpose,
Terri Mongait

ACKNOWLEDGMENTS

I AM GRATEFUL TO ALL THOSE with whom I have had the pleasure to work during this first foray into the world of memoir. I would especially like to thank my husband, Peter, who has stood by me through the roller-coaster ride of my life. He has stayed strong and supportive no matter where I have been in this book-writing process. He has shown me, by his example, what a good partner, and person, should be.

Nobody has been more important to me in the pursuit of this book than the members of my family. I would like to thank my parents, Ann and Ray Cook, whose love and guidance are with me in whatever I pursue. Most importantly, I wish to thank my loving and supportive sister, Claudia, who dropped everything to support me during my TBI accident and who provided some of the life messages that have made me the person I am today. And thank you to my brother, Chris, who has always played in the periphery of my experiences.

Many, many thanks to my editor and writing coach, Donna Mazzitelli of Writing With Donna, for supporting me through this writing and editing process. And finally, to Kirsten Jensen of My Word Publishing for her constant support and hand-holding during this entire publishing process.

This labor of love and inspiration could not have been born without each of the aforementioned family, friends, and colleagues. Gratitude.

ABOUT
THE AUTHOR

TERRI MONGAIT, EGC, CMT, is a certified Equine Gestalt Coach and Canfield Methodology Trainer, transformational speaker, and Equine-Facilitated Success Coach. She is a published author in volume three of  the *Ready to Fly* anthology series, volume one of the *Touched by a Horse* anthology series, and volume one of *To Be Inspired*.

Terri currently lives at Begin Again Ranch in Sedalia, Colorado, with her husband, four horses, one mini-donkey, six chickens, three dogs, and one barn cat. She enjoys her passion for writing, all things Disney, and the opportunity to work with women and couples, helping them to transform their lives and find success on their own life journeys.

To hire Terri, to learn from her and her herd of wisdom horses, or have her speak at your next event, please contact her through her website, www.BeginAgainRanch.com.